Leading Issues in e-Learning Research
MOOCs and Flip:
What's Really Changing?

For researchers, teachers and students

Edited by
Mélanie Ciussi

Leading Issues in e-Learning Research: MOOCs and Flip:
What's Really Changing?
Volume Two

ISBN: 978-1-910309-89-6 (print)
        978-1-910309-90-2 (e-Pub)
        978-1-910309-95-7-(Kindle)

Printed by Lightning Source POD

Published by: Academic Conferences and Publishing International Limited, Reading, RG4 9AY, United Kingdom, info@academic-publishing.org
Available from www.academic-bookshop.com

Contents

About the editor

Dr Mélanie Ciussi holds a PhD in Education Sciences and is Associate Professor of Knowledge Management & Digital Technologies at SKEMA Business School. She is a specialist of mobile learning and pedagogical innovation, and in 2011, was winner of the Apple ARTS prize in support of pedagogical research. In 2013, she was Dean of the European Conference of e-Learning. She also directed a two year research project on serious games for the French Ministry of Research. For five years, Mélanie was responsible for e-learning at CERAM Business School, and has also worked in HR as Assistant Director of Personnel for Marks and Spencer in Scotland and Belgium. Her last book, Leading Issues in e-Learning, vol. 1, is published by Academic Conferences and Publishing International.

List of Contributing Authors

Riana Bester, CTI Education Group, GHO, Johannesburg, South Africa

Carolyn Bilsborow, University of South Australia

William Chang, School of Computing and Information Systems, Athabasca University, Canada

Kathleen Doherty, University of Tasmania, Hobart, Australia

Daniela Gachago, Cape Peninsula University of Technology, Cape Town, South Africa

Kate Galvin, Faculty of Health & Social Care, University of Hull, UK

Maggie Hutchings, Faculty of Health & Social Sciences, Bournemouth University, UK

Eunice Ivala, Cape Peninsula University of Technology, Cape Town, South Africa

Jo-Anne Kelder, University of Tasmania, Hobart, Australia

Carolyn King, University of Tasmania, Hobart, Australia

Kinshuk, School of Computing and Information Systems, Athabasca University, Canada

Marlena Kruger, CTI Education Group, GHO, Johannesburg, South Africa

Ulemu Luhanga, Queen's University, Kingston, Canada

Fran McInerney, Australian Catholic University/Mercy Health, Melbourne, Australia

Rob Phillips, Murdoch University, Perth, Australia

Anne Quinney, Faculty of Health & Social Sciences, Bournemouth University, UK

Brenda Ravenscroft, Queen's University, Kingston, Canada

Andrew Robinson, University of Tasmania, Hobart, Australia

Daniyar Sapargaliyev, Almaty Management University, Kazakhstan

Qing Tan, School of Computing and Information Systems, Athabasca University, Canada

Anton Thiart, Cape Peninsula University of Technology, Cape Town, South Africa

James Vickers, University of Tasmania, Hobart, Australia

Justin Walls, University of Tasmania, Hobart, Australia

Denise Wood, Central Queensland University, University of South Australia and the University of the Western Cape, South Africa iv

Introduction to Leading Issues in e-Learning Research:
MOOCs and Flip: What's Really Changing?

1 Introduction

Three years after Volume 1 of *Leading Issues in e-Learning*, major break-throughs have taken place in the world of education including the arrival of MOOCs and flipped classrooms. A New York Times article declared 2012 to be the *"...year of the MOOC."* Today, massive open online courses (MOOCs) are still giving journalists plenty to write about along with the concept of flipping. Flipping means interactive classes with a teacher, while knowledge is mashed up at home – on or off line (with MOOCs or e-Learning courses, ebooks, traditional media, web resources, etc.).

Now in 2015, we can get some perspective on MOOCs (though this is less true for flipped classrooms). Data are available in diverse publications such as the HarvardX and MITx report on Edx's first year of open online courses (2012-13), or Kizilcec et al's work (2013) on Stanfords' MOOCs. MOOCs promised to educate the world, improve learning for everyone, and all this at no cost to the learner. Has this goal been achieved? Let's take a closer look step by step.

2 Educating the world

Let the figures talk: over 200 universities have created MOOCs and more than 1,200 courses are on offer with an average of nearly two new MOOCs starting every day. 10 million students use MOOCs (as of January 2014) with *Coursera* the predominant platform (47% of providers), accompanied by edX and Udacity. But only a small share of the world's population has accessed MOOC content. Which countries actually benefit from these self-directed online courses?

In terms of the geographical distribution of registered students, Ho et al (2014) rank the top 10 countries by numbers of registered students for all

HarvardX and MITx MOOCs as: the USA (28%), India (13.2%), UK (4.1%), Brazil (3.4%), Canada (2.7%), Spain (2.2%), Russian Federation (2%), Pakistan (1.9%), Germany (1.8%) and Egypt (1.7%). The United Nations' listing of the 49 least developed countries in the world[1] accounted for only 20,745 students or 2.7% of the total. We could argue that it is mainly the US and India benefitting from MOOC education and accessible online course content. But this is not entirely true. The volumes are so large that even less-represented countries still have large numbers enrolled, and this is true for the 20 745 students enrolled from the UN's list of underdeveloped countries. In Spain, the 6th country for registrations, enrolments totalled 16,926 but Spain is also the country with the highest rate of completion and earned certificates (13.74% of all students certified, or 2,400 participants). Next in line is Greece (12%), the Czech Republic (11.8%), Hungary (11%), and so on. It is somewhat surprising that the US and India are not in the top 30 countries in terms of certification rate!

Latest registration for all HarvardX offerings (excluding MITx this time) shows a total of 1,594,960 enrolments across 195 countries - figures that are similar to those cited by Ho (2014). Enrolments are on the increase in the US (+7 percentage points), together with a number of other countries: Canada (+0.7 points), United Kingdom (+0.3 points) and China (+1.4 points). Registrations are decreasing in other parts of the world, notably India, Brazil, Spain, the Russian Federation, Pakistan and Egypt. What does this mean in terms of "learning for everyone"? The trend should be monitored, particularly in less developed countries such as Sudan and Uganda. Between 2012 and 2014 new enrolments in these countries dropped. In Uganda, though, completion rates are higher than in all countries with increased enrolments: 13% against 6% in the US. Is this a confirmed trend? Does it mean that the poorest countries get better certification rates?

To find out, I researched the estimated number of certificates issued worldwide by HarvardX (as of August 2014)[2]. It appears that the countries with highest certification rates are Burkina Faso (24% of enrolments, 54 of 223), Greece (19%), Surinam (15.5%), Cambodia, Benin, Madagascar

---

[1] Site United Nations

[2] http://harvardx.harvard.edu/harvardx-insights/world-map-certificate-attainment

(13.3%), Yemen, Myanmar and Uzbekistan (11%). Based on this, MOOCs are keeping the promise of global access to education.

3 Better learning

Do those who enrol in MOOCs learn better, or more? MOOCs have been challenged regarding their efficacy and role compared with traditional face-to-face university classes.

Ho et al (2014) state that all cohorts learn equally and that MOOCs are more effective than traditional lectures. This is true if they are compared to teacher-centred traditional lectures (transmissive models of teaching). However, if compared with courses taught through active learning or *interactive engagement pedagogy* (Pritchard; in Chandler, 2014) the same does not hold. And this is not surprising. If we examine MOOC history, their ancestors (CD Roms) clearly promised to deliver individually targeted content and course design was either behaviourist and/or constructivist. CD Roms were content-centred, and MOOCs still are (xMOOCs and even cMOOCs!). Proof of this is that, in both cases, students' evaluation of knowledge acquisition remains individual (work/quiz/report). And so are MOOCs about to become the future of education? I think not. They might be the future of content delivery; they might even have a serious impact on lectures delivered in conference halls (the end of endless lectures), but MOOCs will certainly not be the future of education. For one thing, we need face-to-face interaction with a teacher/coach, the lack of which has proved to be a failure (e-Learning in the early years 2000-2005). Even if Web 2.0 has opened up a window for online interaction and virtual sociali-zation, this cannot be compared to a face-to-face course either with active learning or interaction (confirmed by the study of Ho et al). Of course MOOCs (and specifically cMOOCs) can incorporate teamwork, offer discus-sion forums, and encourage social networking groups or collective blogs. But how many participants really learn from overcrowded online forums, where discussions – defined as a minimum 2 turn exchange (Henri, 2008) – are in the minority? How many can benefit from social learning online? For all HarvardX and MITx MOOCs in 2012-13, no more than 5% of learners were accredited and another 5% explored more than half of the course. It is mainly the 5% of accredited learners who participated in forums more than once (on average, half of them). Although this may seem little, it still provides new opportunities to learn for people who would not have ac-cessed prestigious universities. Ho et al (2014) also conclude that,

"...course certifications are misleading and counterproductive indicators of the impact and potential of open online courses." (p. 2). Indeed, browsing a course and just exploring a few modules is part of MOOC design. Free to register, free to browse, free to use. Some may say that the future of MOOCs will be micro MOOCs, or MOOMs (massive open online modules) ... not courses, but rather modules where students can pick and mix what they want to learn. Maybe the future will also give rise to MOOCs built around active and social learning methods, for these already exist – albeit in the minority (project based learning, peer coaching MOOCs).

A fantastic opportunity stemming from MOOCs' focus on content is the increased quality of online resources. Since MOOCs are open and public, they are naturally in the spotlight. They are publicly evaluated by partici-pants and can thus be a fantastic marketing tool for schools. They can likewise be disastrous if not up to standards - institutions will not counte-nance bad press and bad evaluations. This means that they allocate re-sources and budget to their MOOCs and the effect has been to drastically improve online content. As a ripple effect on other teachers in the institu-tion, MOOCs are an accelerator and leverage to e-Learning. Up to date, focus on design, pedagogy sequencing, task orientated, large scale, it has propelled e-Learning to another level (such as Web 2.0 has propelled social learning online).

4   Learning for everyone

Let's look at the subpopulation counts for all HarvardX and MITx MOOCs in 2012-13. In Ho et al (2014) the typical student already holds a bachelor's degree, is aged 26 or older (66% of 841,687) and 29% of total MOOC en-rolments are women. Six per cent are over 50 years old and 1 percent be-low 15. Those who certified (10%) have an average age of 28 and 75% hold a bachelor's degree or above. Emanuel et al (2013) show that 83% of sur-vey respondents taking University of Pennsylvania open online courses have 2 or 4 year college degrees. On HarvardX, the trend is confirmed: 67.2% are bachelor and above. We can say that typical enrolments are young professionals, learning on line in their own time, on their own initia-tive, at their own pace on topics that motivate them. They are in control of their learning and while this is part of the "learning for everyone", MOOCs tend to be for people who are already educated to degree level. So this educational experience is probably complementary to working life and provides opportunities for lifelong learning (Kizilcec et al, 2013). This seems to be consistent with the idea of Micro MOOCs or MOOMs where people choose specific topics of interest (instead of an entire course), and explains the very low completion rates (Koller et al, 2013). Or is that just the way it is now? What if the 26% of enrolments in secondary level increased? Would it be fair to limit the learning experience to a set of micro MOOMs, best suited to young professionals? Learning is not easy, stepping out of a MOOC is. Must everything be "on demand" to facilitate learning?

5 Free courses

Creating a MOOC is labour intensive. Are they reusable at low marginal cost? The free model seems to have confronted against issues concerning return on investment. Ho et al (2014) statistics on active students show that very few students browse the course after it ends. They also argue that content is no longer reusable year after year: the world is changing so quickly that data and videos must be constantly updated.

If MOOCs are definitely part of the big change in the educational world, we must not underestimate the other trends that are equally redesigning the ecosystem today. Flipped classrooms, for example, are a disruptive way to teach: no more content taught in class. To see the challenge raised by flip let's look at both sides of the flip. On one side there are face-to-face classes. If they are more interactive, based on active learning methods, there is little doubt that the learning experience is optimized. Analysis and discussion contribute to solid active learning pedagogy. On the other side of the flip, however, it is not so clear cut: the individual learning at home. But how and where exactly does this take place? At home, in otherwise wasted transportation time? What is the parent's role? How does one know if the student is being conscientious? Most students do not transform into high level scholars at home just because they are doing flipped classrooms.

It is this latter horizon that we address in this book, specific to the context of higher education.

The spirit of this collection is to present the latest issues in digital learning. Each chapter proposes a specific view on distance learning using MOOCs, flip and also gamification or active learning methods using 2.0 tools. The selection favours works that are innovative and complementary. The collection is also both empirical and practical: we have consciously chosen works that advance best practice resulting from experimentation.

The first and second articles focus on MOOCs. The first describes the initial design process as well as the MOOC learning style: to encourage participants to assume the role of reflective practitioners. The second article analyses successful examples of MOOCs in post-Soviet countries and shows the main problems in implementation, as well as the need to create MOOCs for Russian-speaking users. The third and fourth articles focus on flipped classrooms. How effective is the flipped classroom for courses whose learning goals are employability skills such as collaborative learning, writing skills and higher order thinking skills? The next three articles differ from the others by presenting diverse experimentations with smartphone devices and augmented reality tools in formal learning contexts, including one focusing on creative problem-solving. The last article explores strategies for effective change management while minimising risk in digital-transformational-learning contexts. It is an apt conclusion to this book, stressing the need to set up strategies for change as digitalization creates new ways of teaching and learning that impact the entire institution.

These works are derived from the latest research articles published in the *Electronic Journal of e-Learning* and refereed proceedings from the *European Conferences on e-Learning* and the *International Conferences on e-Learning*.

References

Breslow, L., Pritchard, D. E., DeBoer, J., Stump, G. S., Ho, A. D., & Seaton, D. T. (2013) Studying Learning in the Worldwide Classroom Research into edX's First MOOC (Research and Practice in Assessment). Retrieved from http://www.rpajournal.com/dev/wp-content/uploads/2013/05/SF2.pdf

Ciussi, M (2014). What are student's expectations in terms of online learning and pedagogy in general? A longitudinal study, SKEMA Business School, Sophia Antipolis, France

DeBoer, J., Ho, A. D., Stump, G. S., & Breslow, L. (2014). Changing "course": Reconceptualizing educational variables for Massive Open Online Courses. Educational Researcher. Retrieved from Retrieved from http://edr.sagepub.com/content/early/2014/02/06/0013189X14523038.abstract

Ho, A. D., Reich, J., Nesterko, S. O., Seaton, D. T., Mullaney, T., Waldo, J., & Chuang, I. (2014). Harvardx and Mitx: The first year of open online courses (Harvardx and MITx Working Paper No. 1). Retrieved from http://papers.ssrn.com/sol3/papers.cfm?abstract_id=2381263

Hollands, F. and Tirthali, D. (2014) MOOCs: Expectations and Reality, Full report. Center for benefits cost studies of Education, Teachers college, Columbia University Retrieved from http://www.academicpartnerships.com/sites/default/files/MOOCs_Expectations_and_Reality.pdf

Koller, D., Ng, A., Do, C., & Chen, Z. (2013) Retention and Intention in Massive Open Online Courses: In Depth (Educause Review). Retrieved from http://www.educause.edu/ero/article/retention-and-intention-massive-open-online-courses-depth-0

Kizilcec, R. F., Piech, C., & Schneider, E. (2013) Deconstructing Disengagement: Analyzing Learner Subpopulations in Massive Open Online Courses (Proceedings of Learning and Knowledge). Retrieved from http://www.stanford.edu/~cpiech/bio/papers/deconstructingDisengagement.pdf

Nesterko, S. O., Seaton, D. T., Kashin, K., Han, Q., Reich, J., Waldo, J., Chuang I., & Ho, A. D. (2014). World Map of Enrollment (HarvardX Insights). http://harvardx.harvard.edu/harvardx-insights/world-map-enrollment

Nesterko, S. O., Seaton, D. T., Kashin, K., Han, Q., Reich, J., Waldo, J., Chuang I., & Ho, A. D. (2014). Education Levels Composition (HarvardX Insights).

Pritchard D. in Chandler D. L. (2014). Study: online classes really do work. MIT News. Retrieved from http://newsoffice.mit.edu/2014/study-shows-online-courses-effective-0924

Leading Issues in e-Learning Research
MOOCs and Flip: What's Really Changing?

Designing for Quality: The Understanding Dementia MOOC

Carolyn King[1], Jo-Anne Kelder[1], Kathleen Doherty[1], Rob Phillips[2], Fran McInerney[3], Justin Walls[1], Andrew Robinson[1] and James Vickers[1]
[1]University of Tasmania, Hobart, Australia
[2]Murdoch University, Perth, Australia,
[3]Australian Catholic University/Mercy Health, Melbourne, Australia

Originally published in EJEL (2012) Volume 12 Issue 2

Editorial commentary

This chapter describes the initial design process of a MOOC in the public health sector as well as the MOOC learning style, which encourages participants to assume the role of reflective practitioners. The authors employed Laurillard's (2012) framework which connects learning types with digital technologies to help structure a MOOC into diverse activities. For learning through "production", for example, participants had to complete a reflective journal; for learning through "practice", they used an interactive anatomy program; for learning through "reflection," they worked with thought trees. This chapter is particularly useful for those who are planning to create a MOOC. The course described met with great success due to its topic and design. In the first two sessions (July 2013-March 2014), over 24,000 participants registered from around 100 countries, with 38% (or 80% of active participants) completing the course.

Abstract: The introduction of Massive Open Online Courses (Moocs) as a vehicle for education delivery presents opportunities and challenges. In the context of the Wicking Dementia Research and Education Centre (Wicking Centre), the driver to develop a MOOC was the promise of addressing the international deficit in evidence-based dementia education, as well as the lack of research into international perspectives on dementia. The Wicking Centre's activity integrates research and education, framed by the concept of 'quality of life across the trajectory of dementia.' With dementia emerging as the public health issue of the 21st century, lack of dementia education at multiple levels, professional and non-professional, is of increasing concern. The disruptive character of MOOCs, with associated risks and uncertainties, warranted the application of a research-oriented project management approach to development. This included investing resources in gathering and analysing data to underpin each phase of decision-making. We used a design-based research approach incorporating the concept of 'life-cycle of an e-learning design' (Phillips et al. 2012). Data collection and analysis focused on three dynamically interacting components: 1) expertise in dementia knowledge and dementia education; 2) a cohort-centric approach to design and delivery, and 3) models and designs for MOOCs currently promoted, discussed and reported in the higher education discipline. Laurillard's Conversational Framework, relating types of learning, teaching-learning activities and the digital technologies that support them (2012), informed the selection of digital technology elements for massive-scale engagement of our identified cohort. The paper describes the initial design process and the outcomes of the limited release pilot that informed the first full offering of the MOOC.

Keywords: MOOC, Open Education Resources, Dementia, Education, Online Learning, Design

1   Introduction

This paper addresses the design and pilot of a Massive Open Online Course (MOOC) about dementia, an issue of global importance. Dementia refers to a decline in cognitive and behavioural function, primarily as a result of neurodegenerative disease. The trajectory of most dementias is progressive mental and ultimately physical degeneration, leading to death over a variable period, usually 3-8 years from diagnosis. The prevalence of dementia worldwide has sharply increased as populations age, with numbers expected to double by 2030 and triple by 2050 (World Health Organization 2013). In the Australian context, and consistent with these figures, it is estimated that the number of people with dementia will increase from 298,000 to 891,000 from 2011 to 2050 (Australian Institute of Health and Welfare, 2012). To accommodate the care needs of this group, it is estimated that the current aged care workforce in Australia must quadruple (Productivity Commission 2011). There is, therefore, a need to provide quality dementia education for health professionals, care workers and family members who care for people with dementia. A lack of dementia knowledge has the potential to diminish the quality of care, and thus quality of life, for the person diagnosed, particularly at the end of life stage (Mitchell et al., 2004, Di Giulio et al., 2008, Sampson et al., 2005). Caring for people with dementia involves a range of management and decision-making requirements including those associated with diagnosis, health and social support, medical management, carer support, behavioural strategies, psychological and psychiatric care, and palliative and terminal care.

The authors work at, or are otherwise affiliated with, the Wicking Dementia Research and Education Centre (Wicking Centre), Faculty of Health, University of Tasmania. The Wicking Centre integrates expertise in neuroscience, translational dementia research and dementia education. In particular, the educational programs of the Wicking Centre brings together research-based knowledge of the neurobiological basis of dementia with evidence-based approaches to the care of people with dementia. In this regard, care strategies are developed through the prism of dementia as a degenerative, progressive and terminal condition. Recognising that dementia is a problem of global significance, the Wicking Centre sought to extend its reach, and increase the global awareness and understanding of dementia through its educational programs.

The Wicking Centre introduced an Associate Degree in Dementia Care for domestic Australian students in 2012. The course was targeted at non-traditional learners: people primarily employed in the aged care industry as personal and community-based carers for people with dementia. The course was further developed into a fully online Bachelor Degree in Dementia Care, available internationally in 2013. The need for large-scale dementia education delivery, in conjunction with the Wicking Centre's particular expertise in both dementia research (investigating the nature of the disease) and dementia education (providing health professionals with evidence-based knowledge to inform their practice), was a driver for the decision to investigate the new pedagogies and learning platforms being developed in response to the disruptive technology that is MOOCs. Despite the high risk of expending considerable resources to develop a free education service, it was clear that a MOOC design had potential to address the problem of scale, and reduce the education deficit internationally. In par-

3

ticular, it presented an opportunity to serve non-traditional cohorts, particularly care workers and family-based carers, who typically do not have access to formal education opportunities.

2 Open Education and Massive Open Online Courses (MOOCs)

2.1 Open Education

Universities have a long tradition of freely sharing information and knowledge but, over the last century, access to this information has become increasingly restricted due to commercialisation and a market-driven approach to education delivery. The emergence of Internet technologies has enabled increased access to information and knowledge, and various 'open' initiatives have emerged to challenge the restricted commercial model.

At its core, Open Education emphasises the 'public good' over the 'private good'. It provides opportunities to those who find it difficult to access education via traditional channels. This might include people from disadvantaged backgrounds and those in developing countries. However, in addition, a University might adopt Open Education:

- to enhance reputation and attract students
- to apply its expertise to address global problems
- to generate income
- to improve the efficiency of learning and teaching practice
- to improve student learning outcomes (Norton et al, 2013)

The University of Tasmania supported the development of the *Understanding Dementia* MOOC in line with its strategic intention to enhance its reputation in Open Education. The Wicking Centre's rationale for developing the MOOC was to apply its research and education expertise to address a global deficit in dementia knowledge and to enhance its reputation while attracting students into a fee-paying course, the online Bachelor of Dementia Care.

2.2   Massive Open Online Courses

The concept of MOOCs has evolved over recent years. In the original expression of the idea, an open course was offered in a distributed fashion across the Internet, outside the confines of an individual institution, to make it 'massively open'. It was taught collaboratively, with participants and course materials dispersed across the web using a 'connectivist' pedagogy, in an attempt to democratise education and empower people from disadvantaged backgrounds (Downes, 2012). As the use of this term has evolved, it has become known as a cMOOC (Siemens, 2012).

More recently, MOOC has been used to refer to a course offered freely to the world by one institution, sometimes through commercial brokerages such as MITx (subsequently EDx), Coursera and Udacity. The first instances were by high-profile US institutions supported by venture capital. Large enrolments occurred in some cases, and the concept captured the attention of the mainstream press and university decision-makers worldwide. The commercial style of MOOC has been labelled an xMOOC (Siemens, 2012), a reference to the 'x' in the name of some of the early commercial providers.

While MOOCs are a relatively new phenomenon, they build on decades of research into technology-enhanced learning, discussed, for example, in Collis (1996), Harasim et al. (1995), Herrington et al. (2010), Laurillard (1993, 2002, 2012) and Salmon (2000, 2003). A key finding of this body of work is the need for teachers to support students to construct their own knowledge. While online approaches have enriched the experiences of (previously correspondence-based) distance education students, in recent years, they have been extensively used to 'blend' on-campus activities with online activities (Littlejohn and Pegler, 2007), retaining face-to-face facilitation of learning.

Laurillard's Conversational Framework (Laurillard, 2012) represents the different kinds of roles played by teachers and learners. Used as a design analysis tool, the framework exposes the inherent constraints of a MOOC design for student learning. Teacher presence is minimal in a MOOC environment for reasons of cost and scale, and the predominant means of student-teacher interaction are through asynchronous transmission of information provided by the teacher. Embedding opportunities for engagement that enhance interactions between student and student and between student and content can compensate for any perceived learning deficits due to minimal teacher presence, but is difficult to achieve for 'massive' cohorts.

The approach taken in many xMOOCs explicitly replicates a traditional, transmissionist model of classroom practice (Borden, 2012, Knox et al., 2012). As an example, Norvig's (2012) approach to a 100,000-student artificial intelligence MOOC is representative of a minimalist teacher presence. The design of cMOOCs, by contrast, aims to create a MOOC community that leverages the shared knowledge of members, but this relies on the presence of some "more knowledgeable other in the group" (Borden, 2012). This approach requires students to engage collectively in developing shared knowledge but only works if students are motivated and technically competent to use and develop the MOOC environment.

Thus, the characteristics of students who might successfully complete a MOOC is an important consideration in a MOOC design. Completion rates in MOOCs have been reported to be around 4% (Penn Graduate School of Education 2013). Daniel (2012) argues that such completion rates would be of concern to higher education accreditation bodies and distance education providers. The distance education literature recognises that students need self-efficacy and metacognitive skills to succeed in an isolated online environment. Thus, the target audience needs to be clearly understood and assumptions about their capabilities for a MOOC environment aligned with its design.

Norton's (2013) analysis distinguishes between three general types of outcomes sought by students: learning new things; improving employment prospects; and a general broadening of the mind. He subdivides these into 11 components, and analyses which of these can be achieved effectively through a MOOC, vis-a-vis a blended educational environment. This analysis establishes that there are four outcomes that a MOOC may be effective in achieving: vocational knowledge, knowledge for its own sake, formal credentials and evidence of achievement.

Carolyn King et al.

2.3   MOOC Design

2.3.1   Laurillard's (2012) 'Conversational Framework and the Learning Design'

Laurillard's Conversational Framework (2012) provides a way of thinking about learning that accounts for teacher and learner activity, individual and social aspects of learning and the interaction of theory and practice. It represents "the different kinds of roles played by teachers and learners in terms of the requirements derived from conceptual learning, experiential learning, social constructivism, constructionism, and collaborative learning, and the corresponding principles for designing teaching and learning activities in the instructional design literature." (p. 93). The framework was used to inform and evaluate the learning design of the *Understanding Dementia* MOOC.

The Conversational Framework encompasses six types of learning through: acquisition, inquiry, practice, production, discussion and collaboration. Laurillard provides a map of different digital learning technologies that support those ways of learning in (2012, p. 96, Table 6.3). The peculiar affordances and limitations of learning design for a MOOC meant that in the design of *Understanding Dementia*, we focused on learning through acquisition, practice, production and, in a limited way, discussion as shown in Table 1. These are discussed in more detail in Section 3. *Design of the e-learning environment* and summarised in Table 2.

Table 1: Types of Learning and Supporting Digital Technologies (Laurillard 2012, Table 6.3, adapted)

Learning through	Digital Learning Technology that serve them	Learning focus
Acquisition	Reading multimedia, websites, digital documents and resources; listening to podcasts, webcasts; watching animations, videos.	Expert knowledge transmission
Practice	Using models, simulations, microworlds, virtual labs and field trips, online role-play activities	Student practicing knowledge

7

Learning through	Digital Learning Technology that serve them	Learning focus
Production	Producing and storing digital documents, representations of designs, performances, artifacts, animations, models, resources, slideshows, photos, videos, blogs, e-portfolios	Student knowledge codified
Discussion	Online tutorials, seminars, email discussions, discussion groups, discussion forums, web-conferencing tools, synchronous and asynchronous.	Student sharing individual knowledge and perspectives

Learning through discussion includes a teacher "providing stimulus in the form of a question, or issue" and a learner to "modulate their ideas, and generate further ideas and questions" (p.98). Given that online, large-scale discussion is inherently difficult to manage from both delivery and participant perspectives, we successfully trialled a 'discussion-like' forum of providing sentence stems with invitation to "complete the thought". The 'thought tree' was designed to facilitate a collective 'flow' of personal perspectives and understandings surrounding big concepts like 'quality of life' and 'what the nervous system does'. The thought tree concept generated a large body of contributions from participants, achieving its intended purpose of enabling low stakes, large scale sharing of perspectives that could be analysed by the development team and also dementia researchers.

The outcome of learning through inquiry (learning through finding out) is that students "modulate their conceptual organization" (p. 98) through the process of investigation of materials, guided by the teacher. This learning type assumes a level of motivation and self-efficacy from the participants to investigate resources provided and reflect on concepts taught. We assumed high motivation, but low technical and academic literacy for our target participant cohort and therefore did not design for learning through inquiry.

The affordances of the available MOOC platform and the assumptions about the target cohort meant that our understanding of what comprised "collaboration" was challenged. According to Laurillard, collaboration "incorporates learning through discussion, practice and production." (p. 98) Through learners exchanging experiences of learning through practice, as

8

well as products of practice, individual actions are modulated and discussion generated. For participants of the *Understanding Dementia MOOC*, the learning experience of the MOOC functioned as a launchpad for many participants to use the content provided to initiate collaborative activity in their local context.

This may be a function of the intersection between the topic (dementia) and the cohort: over 60% of students in the first release were caring for someone with dementia. It is not surprising that such a group would be highly motivated and able to apply in practice the knowledge acquired from the course. That emergent collaboration activity occurred within localised (geographical) contexts is also a reasonable outworking of the networked nature of marketing we employed. Not for profit organisations dedicated to providing support and information about dementia, as well as aged care facilities, were contacted and agreed to advertise the *Understanding Dementia* MOOC to their mailing list.

2.3.2   Approach to the Learning Design

We approached the design of the MOOC as a 'wicked problem' (Rittel, 1984 [1972]). This concept applies to situations in which a problem cannot be well-defined and decision-making is best approached as a process of inquiry rather than goal-directed problem-solving. The many uncertainties currently associated with MOOCs warranted a research-oriented and iterative approach to design decisions. Thus, the design evolved over time and was open to a range of MOOC styles, educational design methodologies and pedagogies. The iterative reconceptualising of the MOOC took into account competing tensions between MOOC style, expertise of the content developers, proposed target audience and the limitations of the available MOOC platform. Incremental partial solutions with emergent properties were then reflected on and fed into the next iteration of decision-making (Checkland and Scholes, 1999). The iterative process of investigating possibilities for the design of the *Understanding Dementia* MOOC took place over several months. We started with the target audience and desired outcomes. This led us to consider the kinds of expertise we could deliver as content, and that we needed translation of expertise into course content. We also carefully considered how to use the technology platform in ways that would facilitate the participants' role of learner (Laurillard, 2012), in particular, as reflective practitioner (Schön, 1983).

We decided to use a design-based research approach (van den Akker et al., 2006) for the specific learning environment of the *Understanding Dementia* MOOC. The concept of the e-learning design lifecycle described in Phillips et al. (2012) guided our project plan. A learning design has a life cycle from conceptualisation to maturity and is best conducted as an iterative process in which each phase of development is underpinned by data collection to evaluate and refine the design until it is considered mature. This process includes a baseline analysis, pilot phase and delivery phases that are evaluated to inform refinement of the design and enable measurement of effectiveness. The baseline analysis for the MOOC (the analysis that precedes the first phase in a design lifecycle) included online learning design principles and recommendations from publications such as those referenced in the preceding discussion about MOOCs, target audiences as well as Wicking Centre knowledge and expertise. The pilot was completed in June 2013 and the outcomes of the evaluation data fed into the subsequent design.

2.3.3   *Baseline Analysis*
The baseline analysis was important to establish the nature and extent of the education problem that the Wicking Centre was seeking to address and the expectations of potential and identified stakeholders, including the target audience. This analysis informed decisions on the learning design of the MOOC and also provides the benchmark against which the learning outcomes and other effects of the MOOC will be identified and measured. For example, outcomes relate to the project goals including enhancing the reputation of the University, generating income, improving (online) learning and teaching practice, and the dissemination of Wicking Centre's expertise.

2.3.4   *Intended Outcomes and Audience*
The goal of the *Understanding Dementia* MOOC was to provide a foundation-level course that would increase evidence-based knowledge about dementia, internationally. The target audience was deliberately broader than the Wicking Centre's existing Associate Degree in Dementia Care. It was accessible to:
- Those in Australia interested in dementia who might not be prepared to enrol in a fee-paying course;

- Those carers and others across the world who wished to access quality, evidence based information to assist in understanding dementia.

However, identifying the target cohort was initially problematic. It was clear that dementia knowledge could be of general interest to anyone and it was tempting to take a generalist approach: provide a 'wikipedia' on dementia, in the interests of being broadly appealing or non-exclusive. Initial investigations showed that many organisations were delivering high-quality general dementia information online (Pittman et al., 2012). However, no integrated course was available that provided the crucial links between neuroscience and dementia care, with the additional capacity to inform on the key aspects of a palliative approach. We chose to tailor the learning to those for whom this knowledge would have the biggest impact in terms of translation to practice, to drive evidence based dementia care, and to facilitate a broad recognition of the life-limiting nature of the condition. Identification of the target audience (health professionals, aged care workers, personal carers, people with dementia and their families) was key to informing the design and structure of the course. Furthermore, expanding the target audience internationally raised the potential for cross-cultural sharing of dementia care practices. A well-designed MOOC presented an opportunity to share those different perspectives among course participants, thereby increasing and enriching global understanding about dementia.

3 Design of the e-Learning environment

The e-learning environment was designed taking into consideration Laurillard's "Types of Learning and the Different Types of Conventional and Digital Learning Technologies that Serve Them" (2012, Table 6.3, p. 96). For the context of a MOOC, it was decided to prioritise 'learning though Acquisition' with elements of learning by Practice, Production and Discussion. Table 2 sets out the Learning focus, MOOC technology platform functions and Desired Learning Outcome in relation to the selected Learning Types.

Table 2: Laurillard's (2012) Learning Types as designed into the *Understanding Dementia* MOOC

Learning through	Learning focus	MOOC platform technology functions	Desired Learning Outcome: Learner can...
Acquisition	Expert knowledge transmission (brain, disease, person)	Video interviews of experts accompanied by text transcripts; content summaries	Modulate own concept, observe teacher's practice
Practice	Student practicing knowledge	Body Central software, quizzes, learning activities (eg. scenarios/case studies) with hints and instant feedback	Apply core concepts learned and respond to feedback to improve actions (theory into practice)
Production	Student knowledge codified	Completing the final scene within MOOC family scenarios; recording notes in a reflective journal	Consolidate learning via articulating their conceptual understanding and how they have put it into practice
Discussion	Student sharing individual knowledge and perspectives	Thought tree responses to sentence stems. Discussion forums encouraging sharing of experiences, resources and research	Modulate own ideas and generate further ideas and questions

The design of the MOOC balanced considerations of the target audience characteristics and expertise and MOOC platforms to decide on the MOOC style (xMOOC with cMOOC characteristics). Once the MOOC style was settled, other elements of the design were considered: the curriculum (what was to be taught), the learning design (how it was to be taught), the technical platform to be used, and the expertise available (both technical and domain-specific). Each combination of design elements was evaluated for its ability to meet the goals of the project: to provide international access to quality dementia education, raise awareness of dementia as a life-limiting disease of the brain requiring a care response including palliation, and to support the Wicking Centre's ongoing research efforts. A core team of six part-time staff (consisting of a project coordinator/manager, three technical staff, and two media personnel) developed the learning design. Content experts, who contributed material and provided advice on their particular areas of expertise, supported this team. The project coordinator/manager was also involved in all content development, ensuring a consistent approach to material delivery, and alignment of unit objectives with learning activities.

Having identified the broad range of material possible to deliver, we progressively refined the basic content design for the MOOC into three primary themes: 'the brain', 'the diseases' and 'the person'. Within each theme, content expertise was digested and translated into a presentation format that would enable participants to reflect on and apply in their local context. A guiding principle for each module was to inform students of the theory, encourage them to reflect on the theory in their local context, and to feed back their reflections to all MOOC participants. The themes were developed into separate modules, where each module contained several parts. Each part was designed as a single, scrollable HTML page, with several components:

- Video clips of up to thirty minutes in combined duration
- One or more reflective questions, to be entered into a 'journal'
- A quiz about video content
- One or more questions to guide forum discussion
- Other supporting materials

Discussion questions and thought trees were interspersed throughout the modules. Thought trees were used when asking people to reflect upon big concepts. Discussion questions were used for sharing experiences, resources and research. An interactive anatomy program, Body Central, was also used to support learning about brain and neuron structure, as a foundation for understanding the pathology (abnormal anatomy) of the diseases that cause dementia.

The individual components of the learning design are discussed in the following sections.

3.1.1 Video elements
In many XMOOCs, a single academic expert presents the content. The diversity of content here meant that a single academic or even a small group

of experts would be insufficient to present the range of information re-quired. Accordingly, we sought the input of 11 experts, locally and nation-ally, including scientists, clinicians, health care professionals, educators, people with dementia and carers. By including content experts with the capacity to speak on dementia from a wide variety of perspectives, we were able to integrate information across laboratory based research, as well as care practices, otherwise known as a 'bench to bedside' approach.

Online courses and MOOCs have adopted a range of content delivery styles, ranging from the use of graphics tablets, to PowerPoint or Prezi presentations, to paper-based and white-board explanations. Our baseline analysis of the target audience informed the decision to deliver the major-ity of content as interview-style video clips. Of the diversity of styles cur-rently available on the Internet, two particular approaches inspired the format of our video clips: the Khan Academy uses image annotation and diagrams, with interview-style voiceovers (Khan Academy 2011), and mathematician, Dr Keith Devlin's MOOCtalk blog (2014) describes his use of paper-based illustration of examples, captured using an overhead cam-era. The key to Devlin's approach is the presence of hands, which convey important aspects of non-verbal communication. However, the delivery of content via an interview, in the Khan example, encourages an engaging conversational discourse that enables clarification of difficult concepts as one person takes on the role of the participant. Employing the strengths of these two approaches, we chose to use the interview format for most clips, with the addition of an iPad, graphics tablet or widescreen computer monitor for demonstrating images, drawing diagrams, or presenting text to enhance the explanation of certain content. The interviewer adopted the position of the MOOC participant to contextualize the content and regu-late its complexity. Two cameras were used in all videos to add editing flexibility and viewing interest.

3.1.2   User interface elements

In line with the e-learning project management literature, organizations like Open Universities Australia and the University of Phoenix have adopted a standardised curriculum and instruction method to ensure con-sistent quality and to lower costs (Norton, 2013). However, it became evi-dent early in the process of *Understanding Dementia* MOOC development that this approach lacked the flexibility required to accommodate our di-

Carolyn King et al.

verse content. Rather, content delivery was determined by the particular professional discipline of the presenter, their delivery style, the types of supporting resources and the nature of the material. For example, one content expert used role playing to communicate content, another used hand-drawn graphs on an iPad, and yet another used images presented on a wide-screen computer monitor. Our learning design balanced standardisation with flexibility, accommodating diversity of presentation approaches to ensure that the primary focus was on communication effectiveness, whilst maintaining a coherent curriculum.

3.1.3   Interactive elements
There is increasing evidence to support the efficacy of games as learning tools (Grimley et al., 2012, Muntean, 2011) and we followed this approach by developing the interactive anatomy program, *Body Central*. This software, originally designed by the *Understanding Dementia* project coordinator to assist first year nursing and paramedic students to study Bioscience, was adapted for the MOOC to assist participants to learn the basic anatomy of the nervous system. This software was readily configurable by the content developer, with an image uploader, question database, progression editor and mini-games to test knowledge and retention. In a recent trial, the software was demonstrated to improve quiz scores by 80% compared with conventional paper-based study methods (unpublished data).

3.1.4   Reflective elements
The course was structured to encourage participants to assume the role of reflective practitioners (Schön, 1983). The content, presented by experts in their particular fields, was deliberately non-exhaustive to encourage discussion and debate. Dementia is a contentious and emotive area, with divergent opinions on such issues as diagnosis, stigma, rights and care practices. The learning design included a function enabling participants to record their own reflections about case studies and scenarios, while discussion questions were deliberately structured to enable participants to consider divergent approaches, share their own experiences or to research and share, for example, their local circumstances. Furthermore, rather than being a didactic or prescriptive experience, the intention was for the course to provide a 'melting pot' for international perspectives on dementia knowledge and practices.

4   Content and copyright issues

The issue of copyright was a major concern and the project team sought expert advice to ensure content design decisions were legally compliant and aligned with the Open Education principles to which the Wicking Centre subscribed. Australian Universities are subject to more restrictive copyright laws than, for example, those in the United States (Norton, 2013). Teaching resources were, thus, restricted to those already owned by the content developers, those that could be obtained under open licences or those that could be created specifically for the course. This both added to the development cost of the project, and drastically limited the diversity of resources that could be presented. An additional consideration was the Intellectual Property implications of making available Wicking Centre/University of Tasmania content, including potential loss of income opportunity. Nevertheless, a decision was made to release content developed as part of the *Understanding Dementia* MOOC under a Creative Commons Attribution, Non-Commercial, Share-Alike license. This decision allowed for the development of openly accessible content that supported our intended cMOOC approach. However, the approach taken was at odds with the xMOOC aspects of our learning design, as many xMOOCs do not provide content that can be, for example, reused, remixed or repurposed.

5   MOOC platform and course design

The open instance platform available to the project was largely untried for large scale course delivery. The instance was primarily designed for use as an open educational repository, with limited functionality as a learning environment. This posed significant challenges for the *Understanding Dementia* MOOC design. However, positively, it forced the team to start with pedagogy, and adapt existing tools, rather than defaulting to a design approach that used online technologies because they were available, without clear pedagogical justification. In addition, our cohort-centric approach meant that we could not presume a particular level of prior education or any level of technical proficiency.

The learning styles underpinning Laurillard's (2012) Conversational Framework and the digital technologies that serve them (p96) informed design choices to focus on learning through acquisition, practice, production and discussion. Learning through acquisition was prioritized because of a design assumption of low threshold learning capabilities of target student cohort (technical and academic literacy) coupled with the high value of expert content that we wished to make available.

In terms of the interface with students, courses hosted on the closed instance of the platform were structured as a sequential list of content links that were designed to be progressively navigated by students. A decision was made to stylise the interface using html programming such that content was embedded in the familiar surroundings of a scrollable web page design. Colour-coded backgrounds and activity icons were implemented as visual standards to organise the content, while the distinct course units were arranged into separate pages with navigation arrows at the top and bottom of each page to facilitate progression. Each module within a unit could be downloaded as a stand-alone HTML document, with which students can interact offline.

6   Understanding dementia pilot

In line with the e-learning design-based process (Phillips et al., 2012), a pilot was used as the first phase in the design life cycle. The absence of any other courses on the open instance platform allowed us to implement a restricted release with opportunities to test and identify improvements to the platform, as well as refinements to the design.

A 3-week version of the full 11-week course was trialed April-June 2013 as a soft launch with 184 participants, 128 of whom were active in the course. The pilot was particularly useful in identifying a suite of recurring issues relating predominantly to the registration process, site navigation and technical problems. Many of the issues were resolved during the course of the pilot, while others are being negotiated with the commercial provider as part of platform development. Participants suggested a variety of improvements, including the incorporation of bullet-point summaries of video clips, and task completion checklists, both of which will be implemented in the full release. Twenty-seven participants completed the final feedback survey, which gathered a broad range of data relating to course design, structure, content, accessibility and navigability. Our approach to content delivery was rated highly by the majority of participants:

"The range of presenters and presentation styles, eg case histories as well as professionals, gave breadth to the course." (Pilot participant feedback)

"The in-house videos are exceptionally good ... both in content and quality." (Pilot participant feedback).

92% of respondents rated the course as either good or excellent (top two options), while 88% stated that they would be interested in completing the full course based upon their pilot experience.

"This is a fantastic learning opportunity for professionals and families and suffers of Dementia. It is well put together and easy to understand." (Pilot participant feedback)

The pilot data was not intended to mirror our likely audience for the full-release, as participants were primarily recruited from Wicking Centre, School of Medicine and School of Nursing and Midwifery academics and their networks. Interestingly, word of mouth and social media recruited participants from all over Australia, from a diversity of backgrounds and motivations for learning about dementia. These additional participants potentially reflected the anticipated general level of interest and attraction of the *Understanding Dementia* MOOC. The pilot also demonstrated that a range of qualitative and quantitative data can be collected, validating the tradeoff between cost of delivery and benefit to Wicking Centre research.

Several key design elements evolved from the Pilot and were incorporated into the Full Release, reported in Kelder et al. (2013). In summary, the full release learning design introduced:

- glossary of terms
- course overview, profiles page and orientation modules
- content summary slides at the end of each video clip delivering new content
- 'thought trees' to enable students to contribute to discussion forums in a less threatening environment and anonymously
- MOOC family cartoon scenarios to present case studies in a more engaging manner

- questions designed to facilitate review of the content, separated to facilitate navigation
- hints and instant feedback for each question to enable students to evaluate their own learning

7 Conclusions

This paper has presented an education design project undertaken by the Wicking Dementia Research and Education Centre to develop the *Understanding Dementia* MOOC.

Several conclusions can be drawn from the outcomes of the *Understanding Dementia* MOOC development project.

- Value of a theoretical underpinning to the learning design – guiding choice of digital technology elements and providing criteria for evaluating their effectiveness
- Value of a design-based research approach to the learning design – iterative and incremental data collection and analysis directed toward improving the design with opportunity for measuring effectiveness and impact in later design phases
- Importance of resourcing a design-based approach that is evidence based

The baseline analysis, including of the Wicking Centre's research expertise and the target audience, resulted in the decision that the transmissionist, xMOOC style was broadly appropriate, with features of cMOOC incorporated to facilitate and leverage student engagement. The intention was to share the Wicking Centre's knowledge, and encourage participants to apply that knowledge to their own contexts. At the same time, the *Understanding Dementia* MOOC was designed to provide an opportunity to contribute to international approaches to dementia care, through providing a forum for participants to share their experiences within different contexts. This added a connectivist element to the *Understanding Dementia* MOOC design.

Laurillard's (2012) framework connecting learning styles with digital technologies provided a starting point and guidance for decision-making around the structure and processes built into the learning design. The affordances (and limitations) of the technology platform available to deliver a fully online, open access course meant that we could develop a design that focused on enabling individual learning through acquisition. We were further able to design in opportunities for learning through practice, production and discussion to a limited extent. The framework also provided criteria for analysing the effectiveness of the design.

An important driver for developing the MOOC was to leverage the data which could be generated through its delivery. This included supporting discipline research into international perspectives on dementia care in general, and evaluating the impact of the Wicking Centre's expert content. In addition, the data collected was intended to support research into the scholarship of learning and teaching in the MOOC context. The inclusion of research as an output of the MOOC was agreed with the understanding that this would imply and require a higher contribution of staff time to manage interactions and viewpoints than is usual in xMOOCs. A purposeful tradeoff was thus made between unfunded teaching costs and the potential research outputs.

Of the four effective uses of MOOCs identified by Norton et al. (2013), the *Understanding Dementia* MOOC was initially designed to achieve vocational knowledge and knowledge for its own sake. However, the course has recently been incorporated into a pathway for formal credentials and evidence of achievement, via articulation with an elective unit in the Wicking Centre's fully online Bachelor Degree in Dementia Care. Evidence of the success of our design approach is demonstrated by the high rate of MOOC completion (39% of registrants) and subsequent transition of 273 participants into the Bachelor of Dementia Care course.

References

Australian Institute of Health and Welfare 2012. Dementia in Australia, Cat. No. AGE 70. Canberra: Australian Institute of Health and Welfare.

Borden, J. 2012. Flipping The MOOC? FWD.PEARSON.COM [Online]. Available: http://fwd.pearson.com/2012/09/27/flipping-the-MOOC/ [Accessed 7 May 2013].

Checkland, P. & Scholes, J. 1999. Soft Systems Methodology in Action (including a 30- year retrospective), Chitchester, John Wiley and Sons.

Carolyn King et al.

Collis, B. 1996. Tele-learning in a Digital World: The Future of Distance Learning, International Thomson Computer Press.

Daniel, J. 2012. Making Sense of MOOCs: Musings in a Maze of Myth, Paradox and Possibility. Journal of Interactive Media in Education, 2012.

Devlin, K. 2014. MOOCtalk: Let's teach the world [Online]. Available: http://MOOCtalk.org/ [Accessed January 2013].

Di Giulio, P., Toscani, F., Villani, D., Brunelli, C., Gentile, S. & Spadin, P. 2008. Dying with Advanced Dementia in Long-Term Care Geriatric Institutions: A Retrospective Study. Journal of Palliative Medicine, 11, 1023-8.

Downes, S. 2012. Connectivism and Connective Knowledge: Essays on meaning and learning networks. National Research Council, Canada.

Grimley, M., Green, R., Nilsen, T. & Thompson, D. 2012. Comparing Computer Game and Traditional Lecture Using Experience Ratings From High and Low Achieving Students. Australasian Journal of Educational Technology, 28, 619-638.

Harasim, L., Hiltz, S. R., Teles, L. & Turoff, M. 1995. Learning Networks- a Field Guide to Teaching and Learning Online, Cambridge Massachusetts, The MIT Press.

Herrington, J., Reeves, T. C. & Oliver, R. 2010. A guide to authentic e-learning, New York and London, Routledge.

Khan Academy 2011. Cervical Spine Protection in Airway Management (not a substitute for formal training), [Online], Available: https://www.youtube.com/watch?feature=player_embedded&v=DJY89_jC_ZY. [Accessed 6 January 2014]

Knox, J., Bayne, S., Macleod, H., Ross, J. & Sinclair, C. 2012. MOOC pedagogy: the challenges of developing for Coursera [Online]. Association for Learning Technology. Available: http://newsletter.alt.ac.uk/2012/08/MOOC-pedagogy-the-challenges-of-developing-for-coursera/ [Accessed 7 May 2013].

Laurillard, D. 1993. Rethinking University Teaching: A Framework for the Effective Use of Educational Technology, London, Routledge.

Laurillard, D. 2002. Rethinking university teaching: A conversational framework for the effective use of learning technologies (2nd ed.), London, Routledge.

Laurillard, D. 2012. Teaching as a Design Science: building pedagogical patterns for learning and technology, New York, Routledge.

Littlejohn, A. & Pegler, C. 2007. Preparing for blended e-learning, Abingdon, U.K., Routledge.

Mitchell, S., Kiely, D. & Hamel, M. 2004. Dying with Advanced Dementia in the Nursing Home. Archives of Internal Medicine, 164.

Muntean, C. I. Raising Engagement in E-Learning Through Gamification. 6th International Conference on Virtual Learning ICVL, 28-29 October 2011 2011 Cluj-Napoca, Romania 323-329.

21

Norton, A. 2013. The online evolution: when technology meets tradition in higher education. The Grattan Institute.

Norvig, P. 2012. Peter Norvig: The 100,000-student classroom [Online]. Available: http://www.ted.com/talks/peter_norvig_the_100_000_student_classroom.ht ml [Accessed 9 May 2013].

Penn Graduate School of Education Press Room 2013. Penn GSE Study Shows MOOCs Have Relatively Few Active Users, With Only a Few Persisting to Course End [Online]. Available: http://www.gse.upenn.edu/pressroom/press-releases/2013/12/penn-gse-study-shows-MOOCs-have-relatively-few-active-users-only-few-persisti [Accessed January 2013].

Phillips, R., Mcnaught, C. & Kennedy, G. 2012. Evaluating e-learning: guiding re-search and practice, New York, Routledge.

Pittman, N., Vickers, J., Robinson, A., Walls, J., King, C., Carew, T., Padgett, L., Canty, A. & Kelder, J.-A. 2012. Understanding Dementia MOOC Business Case. University of Tasmania.

Rittel, H. W. J. 1984 [1972]. "Second Generation Design Methods"; Interview in: Design Methods Group 5th Anniversary Report: DMG Occasional Paper, 1, 5-10. Reprinted in. In: CROSS, N. (ed.) Developments in Design Methodology. Chichester: Wiley and Sons.

Salmon, G. 2000. E-moderating: the key to teaching and learning online, London, Kogan Page.

Salmon, G. 2003. E-moderating : the key to teaching and learning online, London ; New York, RoutledgeFalmer.

Sampson, E., Ritchie, C., Lai, R., Raven, P. & Blanchard, M. 2005. A Systematic Review of the Scientific Evidence for the Efficacy of a Palliative Care Approach in Advanced Dementia. International Psychogeriatrics: The Official Journal of The International Psychogeriatric Association, 17, 31-40.

Schön, D. A. 1983. The Reflective Practitioner: How Professionals Think In Action, New York, Basic Books.

Siemens, G. 2012. MOOCs are really a platform. ElearnSpace [Online]. Available: http://www.elearnspace.org/blog/2012/07/25/MOOCs-are-really-a-platform/ [Accessed 7 May 2013].

Van Den Akker, J., Gravemeijer, K., Mckenney, S. & Nieveen, N. (eds.) 2006. Educational design research, Abingdon, U.K.: Routledge.

Forced Necessity: Moocs in Post-Soviet Countries

Daniyar Sapargaliyev
Almaty Management University, Kazakhstan
Originally published in the Proceedings of ICEL 2014

Editorial commentary

This chapter presents the challenges of introducing MOOCs in countries like Russia, the Ukraine and Kazakhstan. Sapargaliyev presents diverse MOOC projects which sometimes face legal issues as MOOCs sometimes fit poorly with national educational standards / regulations. Moreover, some universities question the motive behind investment in MOOCs. The author also points out that the lack of MOOCs taught in local languages (e.g., Ukrainian, Kazakh, and Belarusian) is problematic. This is a growing issue in global education and challenge somewhat MOOCs' claims in terms of educating the world. The majority of courses are in English and this excludes most of the world's population: only about 6% of the planet's population are native English speakers. In November 2014, for example, HarvardX registered 12,500 Ukrainians (0.7% of all participants) and 23,600 Russians (1.3% of all participants).

Abstract: This article describes the current state and development of Massive Open Online Courses (MOOCs) in different post-Soviet countries. Today MOOCs is one of the most popular and growing educational trends. In general, MOOCs are supported and developed only in developed countries. At the same time, MOOCs are partly implemented in developing countries (such as Russia, Ukraine, Kazakhstan and other). We can observe the first stages in the introduction of online courses in post-Soviet countries. In this article, we will describe some successful examples of MOOCs and will show the main problems in implementation of the massive open online courses. We found that some Russian and Ukrainian scientists have successfully implemented MOOCs in their universities. However, the large-scale distribution of MOOCs is not possible in these countries yet. In recent years there were presented some new platforms for open online courses. Leading Russian universities have introduced the first massive open online courses for Russian-speaking users. Nevertheless, there are still many challenges abd barriers in the implementation of the MOOCs. The legislation of higher education system is still not ready for new standards of online learning platforms. We hope that our future research will demonstrate results of development the national platforms for the MOOCs in post-Soviet countries.

Keywords: MOOC, developing countries, Russia, Ukraine, higher education

1   Introduction

The Massive Open Online Courses (MOOCs) become a very popular and controversial phenomenon in higher education of the Western World. In the same time, new technological and educational opportunities and platforms are still not available in post-Soviet countries.

The first experiment on the implementation of MOOCs has already carried out in the Commonwealth of Independent States (CIS). For example, Kukharenko (2013a) has conducted the experimental online course: "Development of e-Learning strategy in organization" for teachers from Ukraine, Russia and other countries in 2011. Though only 45 learners participated in this MOOC from different countries, the results showed that "MOOC is new and not always obvious concept; idea causes great difficulties for participants from CIS" (Kukharenko, 2013b, p.275).

Some Russian universities have started to participate in international projects implementing MOOCs. In early 2013, European Association of Distance Teaching Universities launched the first pan-European MOOCs and only one partner (Moscow State University of Economics, Statistics and Informatics) in this project was from Russia (European Commission, 2013).

The purpose of this study is demonstration of successful examples of MOOCs in Russia and other post-Soviet countries. We have analyzed Russian-language academic sources about the development of MOOCs in post-Soviet countries. We have identified the main barriers in development of MOOCs in this region. Also we will offer possible solutions to improve this situation in the future.

2 Development of MOOCs

Today only two post-Soviet countries, Russia and Ukraine demonstrate educational potential for development of MOOCs. Perhaps the main reason of this situation is that these countries have large population (totally about 200 million people) and promising market in online learning.

Many Russian scientists have analysed the prospects of MOOCs and its potential in higher education (Artushevskaya, 2013; Bogdanova, 2013a; Bogdanova, 2013b; Popov & Cherkasova, 2013). Nevertheless MOOCs are still not provided in Russian higher education. Massive open online courses' platforms are not fit to national educational standards. Moreover, some leading experts argue that MOOCs can threaten national security in educational area. Though many Russian universities are technologically ready to implement MOOCs, but legislation base is still needed in improvement (Goretkina, 2013). But in some cases, MOOCs successfully use for studying English and help Russian students in deeper understanding of different aspects of the language learning (Kokorina, 2013).

The Ukrainian researcher Kukharenko (2012) conducted one of the first MOOC in post-Soviet countries. The main purpose of his course "Distance learning: from A to Z" was to analyse the development of distance learning in Ukraine. Course participants noted that MOOC had constant access to educational materials at any time and offered possibilities for sharing educational resources among all learners. Meanwhile, Panchenko (2013) identified the future potential of MOOCs for Ukrainian universities and considered MOOC certificates as a completion of advanced training courses. Another Ukrainian researcher Bugaychuk (2013) in his work examined the typology, history and future development of MOOCs in post-Soviet countries. Also, Bugaychuk (2012) had formulated principles of teaching in MOOC and outlined the main directions of MOOC's development in Ukraine.

As we can see, the development of massive open online courses is at an early stage. However, MOOCs have great potential for expansion in the Commonwealth of Independent States.

3 Russian language MOOCs

One of the ambitious Russian language MOOC projects is "Universarium" (www.universarium.org). This online platform was launched in December 2013. Today about 35,000 participants have been enrolled to the Universarium courses. But the leading Russian universities are still not hurry to cooperate with the project. All courses have created by the leading professors from famous Russian universities (such as Moscow State University and Moscow Physical-Technical Institute). The project developers are planning to enter to European educational market by presenting new courses in English language. Also, future participants of the Universarium will receive official State certificate. The main obstacles in the adaptation of this MOOC platform in Russia are the inertia of academic environment and absence of online education culture (Bulin, 2014).

The Russian MOOC project "Eduson.tv" consists of professional video lectures on the business topics. This web service is intended for a user who can not afford to complete MBA course. Today the platform is available in Portuguese, Russian, English and Chinese languages. Most of learners are citizens of BRIC (acronym that refers to Brazil, Russia, India and China). The first lecture of each 25 courses is always free, but then a learner has to pay for continue of the course. One of the innovate features in Eduson platform is interactive and non-linear video lecture. Each course simulates a job interview. The platform shows the next piece of video depending on a learner answers. Each user can end the "job interview" as a failure or with high salary results (Eduson, 2013).

The other Russian language platform of online learning is "Uniweb" (www.uniweb.ru). This web service cooperates with more than 10 Russian universities. This platform uses different distance methods of education that try to repeat the process of full-time and face to face learning. Developers of the platform argue that "Uniweb" is not online course platform and they are trying to implement formal educational programs in new online learning formats (Uniweb, 2013).

We have shown only a few MOOC projects in Russian language. We believe that these platforms will be popular among Russian-speaking users in the nearest future.

4 Problems and challenges

The main problems in implementation of MOOCs have been studied by a number of Russian-speaking researchers. For example, Andreev (2013) argues that MOOCs still do not exist in Russia. There are only a few examples of free and open online educational courses (proto MOOCs). Most of these proto courses have access to theoretical materials in text and graphical forms. Also there is lack of communication between the students and teachers' consultations.

Other Russian scientist Bebnev (2013) has the similar opinion. The author has studied some experiences of private MOOC projects that did not achieve any impressive success. The Russian universities are usually very far from a dialogue with educational startups and do not understand the motives for investment in online learning platforms.

As we have seen the implementation of MOOCs in post-Soviet countries is still at an early stage of development and it requires significant resources to successfully continuation. One of the main problems in promoting MOOCs in post-Soviet countries is the lack of courses in local languages (Ukrainian, Kazakh, Belarusian and others). The other significant problem is the status of online learning that is not defined in these countries. Many universities do not recognize the legitimacy of learning with new technologies.

We think that Russian researchers should continue to study the problems and barriers of online learning and determine the potential of MOOCs in the post-Soviet countries.

5 Discussion

In our study, we tried to reflect different aspects of MOOCs' implementation in different post-Soviet countries. However, we were able to show the emergence and development of MOOCs only in Russia and Ukraine. This is due to the fact that scientific works devoted to MOOCs in other CIS are still not reflected in the Russian and English academic literature. However, in the near future, we expect rapid development of MOOCs in Central Asian and Caucasus countries.

We think that MOOCs are well suited for the post-Soviet space. For example, the huge distances between cities in Russia and Kazakhstan are not allowed to have equal access to higher education. The citizens of these countries can have access to quality higher education by the MOOCs that will greatly improve the economic growth in the region.

However, the main problem is that the Russian MOOCs developers can not find leading experts and professors who able to compete with their English-speaking colleagues from developed countries. On the other hand, Russian developers are trying to find their own approaches to the creation of new learning platforms. As we see from the examples, many universities need to find own spaces in the global higher education market. Nevertheless, the problems remain unresolved in legislative frameworks. Many post-Soviet universities have good technological and resource bases for the implementation of online courses. However, national educational standards are not ready for online courses. We hope that in the nearest future, universities will overcome the restrictive laws and develop high-quality online courses in all post-Soviet countries.

References

Andreev, A. (2013) "Pedagogicheskiye aspekty pri obuchenii v MOOC" [Pedagogical aspects in MOOC's learning], *e-Learning World*, [online], www.elw.ru/reviews/detail/6271.

Artushevskaya, S. (2013) "MOOCs v kontekste formirovaniya globalnogo informacionnogo obshestva" [MOOCs in context of forming global information society], *Psychology and pedagogy: methods and problems of practical application,* No. 31, 88-98.

Bebnev, A. (2013) "MOOCs kak novaya innovacionnaya tendenciya obrazovatelnoy sfery" [MOOCs as a new innovation tendency of educational sphere], *Modern problems of science and education,* No. 6.

Bogdanova, D. (2013a) "A Great Breakthrough: from Open Educational Resources to Open Online Courses for the Masses", *Distance and virtual learning,* No. 4 (70), 35-47.

Bogdanova, D. (2013b) "Instructional design elements in modern massive open online courses", *Scientific proceedings,* No. 1 (11), 67-71.

Bugaychuk, K. (2012) "Mass open online courses: concepts, features and prospects of the use in educational process of MIA", *Information Technologies and Learning Tools,* No. 26 (6).

Bugaychuk, K. (2013) "Massive open online courses: history, typology, perspectives", *Higher education in Russia,* No. 3, pp 148-155.

Daniyar Sapargaliyev

Bulin, D. (2014) "Kak besplatno pouchitsya v MGU, Harvarde I gde ugodno" [How to learn for free at MSU, Harvard and anywhere], [online], www.bbc.co.uk/russian/science/2014/01/140122_russia_online_education.sht ml

Goretkina, E. (2013) "Massovoye onlaynovoye obucheniye brosayet vyzov rossiy-skoy sisteme obrazovaniya" [Massive online learning challenges the Russian education system], *PC Week. Russian Edition.* No. 20 (840), www.pcweek.ru/idea/article/detail.php?ID=152251.

Eduson. (2013) About us, [online], www.eduson.tv/about

European Commission. (2013) "Androulla Vassiliou welcomes launch of first pan-European university MOOCs (massive open online courses)", [online], www.ec.europa.eu/education/news/20130423_en.htm.

Kokorina, O.S. (2013) "Collaborative English Language Teaching in Massive Open Online Courses", *Proceedings of the Annual International Conference on Actual Problems of German, Romance and Russian studies,* www.ifl.uspu.ru/images/stories/books/sbornik_2013_2.pdf#page=106.

Kukharenko, V. (2012) "Distancionnoye obycheniye ot A do Ya" [Distance learning from A to Z]

e-Learning World, [online], www.elw.ru/practice/detail/1965.

Kukharenko, V. (2013a) "Innovacii v e-Learning: massoviy otkrytiy distancionniy kurs" [Massive open online course], *Higher education in Russia,* No.10, pp 93-99.

Kukharenko, V. (2013b) "Designing Massive Open Online Courses", [online], Pro-ceedings of the 9th International Conference on ICT in Education, Research and Industrial Applications: Integration, Harmonization and Knowledge Transfer, *www.ceur-ws.org/Vol-1000/ICTERI-2013-p-273-280.pdf.*

Panchenko, L. (2013) "Massive open online course as an alternative way of ad-vanced training for higher educational establishment professors", *Education and pedagogical sciences,* No. 1 (156).

Popov, P. and Cherkasova, I. (2013) "Possibilities of remote educational technolo-gies on the basis of Moodle, Adobe connect, MOOCs in development of innova-tive thinking of subjects of educational space", *Modern problems of science and education,* No. 3.

Uniweb. (2013) About project, [online], www.uniweb.ru/about.

Developing Employability Skills in Humanities and Social Sciences Using the Flipped Model

Brenda Ravenscroft and Ulemu Luhanga
Queen's University, Kingston, Canada
Originally published in the Proceedings of ICEL 2014

Editorial commentary
This chapter proposes the "flipped model" as a method for enhancing learning effectiveness. It offers a significant review of the literature comparing blended and face-to-face learning strategies, and describes an experiment carried out on four flipped courses with an average of 3,370 enrolments. Online resources were used to transmit concepts and information, while class time was used to apply, integrate and synthesize knowledge through small group activities. Results on transversal skills - such as collaboration - and higher order thinking showed positive effects. Students also scored higher in flipped than in traditional lectures, suggesting that blended learning methods can be efficient if face to face sessions involve active learning.

Abstract: Canada, as elsewhere, is experiencing a growing demand for accountability in the higher education sector, and universities are being pressured to provide evidence that they are preparing their graduates for the workforce. In Ontario, Canada's most populous province, the Ministry responsible for higher education has articulated the "essential employability skills" required for graduates; these include communication skills, critical thinking and problem solving skills, and interpersonal skills. Through accreditation requirements, professional programs in business, health sciences and engineering have developed graduate-level competencies and embedded them into their curriculum, but the emerging need to demonstrate these skills in graduates from traditional liberal arts and science disciplines, presents bigger challenges. Even if agreement can be reached about the specific qualities humanities graduates might need in the workplace, other questions remain. How can these skills be developed in subjects that lack clear practical applications? And how can skills be fostered when first- and second-year university courses often have very high enrolments and are commonly taught in large lecture format? This case study examines how the flipped classroom model is providing students with greater opportunities to develop employability skills in humanities and social science courses. Four high-enrolment, introductory courses—psychology, sociology, classics, and gender studies—have been redesigned from traditional lecture format into flipped classroom models with the goal of enhancing student engagement through active learning. By replacing some lecture time with online learning, the courses are able to focus face-to-face learning activities on group work, collaborative learning and the application of knowledge. The effectiveness of these course transformations is being examined through a longitudinal descriptive research study that examines whether students engage in their learning differently in flipped courses. Quantitative data was collected via student surveys in the last offerings of the traditional format courses and is being gathered with each flipped classroom offering, using the Student Class-Level Survey of Student Engagement (CLASSE). Independent sample T-tests of the data for each course show that average scores in the flipped-format courses are higher than in the traditional versions. Specifically, the majority of the courses show statistically significant ($p < 0.05$) improvements in areas associated with employability skills such as collaborative learning, writing skills and higher order thinking skills. The results of this research verify the importance of instructional strategies and course design in achieving the development of employability skills, and suggest that the flipped classroom model can enable this process. By examining the specific ways in which these courses were transformed in the light of the corresponding research results, this paper offers other institutions insights into how to promote the development of similar skills in courses the humanities and social sciences. The demand for institutions of higher education to demonstrate that their graduates have acquired employability skills is a relevant issue across the globe. While much of the discussion has been focused on professional disciplines, this paper presents insights and research into developing these skills in humanities and social sciences.

Keywords: flipped, blended, course design, employability skills, humanities, social sciences

1 Background

Canada, like other countries across the globe, is experiencing a growing demand for accountability in the higher education sector, and universities are being pressured to provide evidence that they are preparing their graduates for the workforce. In Ontario, Canada's most populous province, the Ministry responsible for higher education has articulated the "essential employability skills" required for graduates; these include communication skills, critical thinking and problem solving skills such as analysis, synthesis and evaluation, and interpersonal skills such as team work, leadership and conflict resolution (*Essential Employability Skills*, 2009). In November 2013 the Government of Canada made a commitment to fund a Centre for Skills and Post-Secondary Education set up by the *Conference Board of Canada*, a research organization specializing in economic trends, organizational performance and public policy issues. The *Conference Board* itself has already identified 3 categories of skills needed "to progress in the world of work": fundamental skills (including communication, information management, numeracy and problem solving), personal management skills (such as a positive attitude and responsibility), and teamwork skills like providing feedback in a constructive manner, and leading or supporting when appropriate (*Employability Skills*, 2014).

Through requirements established by accrediting bodies, professional programs in business, health sciences and engineering have developed graduate-level competencies and embedded them into their curricula. However, the emerging need to demonstrate these skills in graduates from traditional liberal arts and science disciplines presents bigger challenges. Even if agreement can be reached about the specific qualities humanities graduates might need in the workplace, other questions remain. How can these skills be developed in subjects that lack clear practical applications? And how can skills be introduced and fostered when first- and second-year university courses often have very high enrolments and are commonly taught in large lecture format? Skills such as being able to work collaboratively in a team require students to work regularly in small groups on specific tasks, and higher order learning skills such as critical thinking and problem solving require activity-based instructional strategies, not lectures. In other words, to instill employability skills in our students, they need to be engaged in active learning educational experiences.

While large lectures may be an efficient way to teach large numbers of students, research shows that lecture formats where students are passive auditors result in fluctuating levels of student attention and low levels of engagement (Middendorf and Kalish, 1996). Passive learning is not effective since it does not enable conceptual understanding and therefore does

Brenda Ravenscroft and Ulemu Luhanga

not lead to long-term knowledge retention (Michael, 2006; Wirth, 2007; Minhas et al, 2012). Furthermore, passive learning does not generally provide students with opportunities to develop higher order thinking skills.

Over the past decade institutions have started to redesign courses to address these challenges (Twigg, 2000). Drawing on research related to how students learn and innovative approaches to instruction (Ambrose, 2010; Mayer, 2008), redesigned courses blend educational technology with improved in-class instructional approaches to enhance the quality of student learning and to improve student success. Vaughan (2007) identified a number of benefits to redesigning courses using a blended learning approach. Since a blended learning approach involves the integration of face-to-face and online learning activities within a course, this approach promotes increased time flexibility for both students and faculty. Furthermore, other benefits of a blended approach to learning include increased student engagement in learning and enhanced student-faculty interaction (Vaughan, 2007). By moving the transmission of information online, classroom time can be focused on active learning, where concepts are applied and knowledge is integrated through group work and problem solving. This blended model of course design is also known as the "flipped" model because of the inversion of the traditional relationship between classroom instruction and homework application.

Carle et al (2009) conducted a small-scale study to examine whether adopting a blended learning approach improved student engagement and academic achievement. Using 30 items from the Class-Level Survey of Student Engagement (CLASSE) to measure student engagement and grades to measure academic achievement, independent sample T-tests were used to examine changes in engagement and achievement across two groups: the control group consisted of students in a section that used a traditional lecture model of teaching and students in a section that adopted a blended approach were the treatment group. Across the 30 CLASSE items, students in the blended learning section indicated greater levels of engagement than students in the traditional section. Furthermore, students in the blended learning section also demonstrated greater and statistically significant average achievement scores in comparison to those in the traditional section (Carle et al, 2009).

33

The following year, Means et al (2010) published a report that included a meta-analysis conducted to compare the effectiveness of online, face-to-face (traditional lecture) and blended learning approaches. The meta-analysis included empirical studies from 1996 to 2008. Forty-five studies were included in the meta-analysis and provided 50 independent effect sizes (27 effect sizes compared online versus face-to-face learning while 23 effect sizes compared blended versus face-to-face learning). Out of this subset of 45 studies, learners in 40 of these studies included undergraduates from across a range of disciplines including languages, science, and social science. In the case of the 23 studies that compared blended versus traditional face-to-face approaches, results of the meta-analysis found that, on average, learning outcomes for students taught using a blended approach were significantly ($p < .001$) better than those of students taught using a traditional face-to-face approach (Means et al 2010).

While the studies by Carle et al (2009) and Means et al (2010) focus on examining the effectiveness of instructor-led course redesign initiatives, Vaughan (2010) presents an institutional course redesign initiative, the Inquiry Through Blended Learning (ITBL) program, created to support faculty engaged in blended learning. The goal of the ITBL program is to "shift teaching and learning from an essentially passive lecture approach to an engaged and collaborative one" (Vaughan, 2010, p 60). Evaluation of the program includes using a combination of faculty interviews and student surveys. The student survey consists of items from three of the five National Survey of Student Engagement (NSSE) survey benchmarks: active and collaborative learning, student interactions with faculty members, and level of academic challenge. The items selected from the NSSE are similar to those found in the CLASSE. To highlight the importance of recognizing course redesign for blended learning as an on-going process, Vaughan (2010) describes how an instructor teaching a third-year course used results from student surveys to make changes to their course. Changes made to the course based on results from student surveys resulted in not only significant improvements in aspects of student engagement (e.g. active and collaborative learning) but also showed increased success and retention rates as evidenced through student grade distributions.

2 Context

Similar to the ITBL program, the Course Redesign Project on which this case study is focused, is a university funded multi-year initiative in the Faculty of Arts and Science, designed to enhance student engagement and to improve student learning in large, introductory courses. The project uses the flipped model to focus class time on engagement through active learning, and follows Garrison and Vaughn's description of blended learning as the purposeful integration of face-to-face and online learning activities (Garrison and Vaughn, 2008). Courses involved in the project represent a range of disciplines, including the sciences, social sciences, arts and humanities; they are selected through a proposal submission process and require a commitment not only from a faculty member (or team), but also from the department. Selected proposals receive funding and consulting resources related to instructional design and instructional technology, and receive integrated supported from the Faculty's Associate Dean (Teaching and Learning). The potential impact of the course redesign project is high: most of the courses serve as gateways to upper-year concentrations, with individual course enrolments ranging from 300 to 1,800 students.

Longitudinal data are being gathered to evaluate the effectiveness of the course transformations on student engagement, approach to learning and knowledge retention. As part of the longitudinal data collection, baseline evaluations are completed prior to the redesign, and data collection will continue for three years thereafter. Ethics approval received for this project also allows access to demographic and student performance data for further analysis.

This case study examines the effect that the Course Redesign Project has had on engagement scores related to employability skills in four high-enrolment, introductory courses—psychology, sociology, classics and gender studies. The paper reports on the curriculum innovations and the impact on student engagement, and discusses the potential for using the flipped model to develop employability skills in social science and humanities courses.

3 Curriculum innovations

The introductory psychology course led the curriculum innovation by being redesigned in 2010/11 and offered as a flipped model in 2011/12. That same year, introductory courses in sociology, classics and gender studies underwent similar redesigns and were offered for the first time as flipped models in 2012/13. Together, the four flipped courses represent an average annual total of 3,370 enrolments. Although the specific design of each course is unique, all of them employ online resources to assist with the transmission of concepts and information, and focus classroom time on applying, integrating and synthesizing knowledge through carefully designed small group activities. To illustrate the variety of curriculum innovations adopted by instructors, details for the four courses are described below.

3.1 Psychology

The largest course in the university, *Principles of Psychology*, serves as the gateway course for concentrations in Psychology, as a requirement for students who go on to complete an Education degree, and as a popular elective course. Lasting the full academic year, PSYC 100 is a 6.0-unit, two-term course offered by the Psychology Department. The traditional course was team-taught by 6 instructors, and required each student to attend two 1.5-hour lectures per week (in sections of 450 students), with the option of attending one teaching assistant-led tutorial per week.

In the 2011/2012 academic year, the course instructors began the initial phase of converting the course to a blended learning, flipped format. In addition to completing work online and through readings, the flipped course required each student to attend a single weekly one-hour lecture led by an instructor (in four sections of 450 students), as well as a one-hour group learning lab (sections of 30 students). In the learning labs students worked on activities in groups of 5, facilitated by undergraduate and graduate teaching assistants.

3.2 Sociology

Introduction to Sociology is a 6.0-unit, two-term course in the Department of Sociology. It acts as the first-year gateway course for concentrations in Sociology, and as an elective for students in other concentrations. The traditional course, taught by a single instructor, required each student to attend two one-hour lectures per week in one of two large sections (400 students), as well as to participate in a one-hour tutorial of 27 students led by a teaching assistant.

In the 2012/2013 academic year, the course instructor began the initial phase of flipping the course. In addition to completing work online and through readings, the blended course required each student to attend a weekly one-hour interactive lecture led by the instructor (in six sections of 145 students), as well as a one-hour group learning lab (sections of 22 students), where students worked on activities in groups of 5, facilitated by graduate teaching assistants.

3.3   Classics

Ancient Humour is a 3.0-unit, one-term course in the Department of Classics. It has a prerequisite of Year 2 standing and serves as an option course for Classics concentrators and an elective course for students in other concentrations. The traditional course, which attracted an enrolment of 410 students, required each student to attend two 1.5-hour lectures per week in a single large section taught by the instructor of the course.

In the 2012/13 academic year, the course instructor began the initial phase of converting the course to a blended learning format. In addition to completing work online and through readings, the flipped course required each student to attend one hour-long, facilitated active-learning lab per week. There were also two hour-long lectures by the instructor, which took place in the first week and the last week of the term in a single large section of 560 students. Group learning labs, with 40 students working in groups of 8, were facilitated by teaching assistants and attended by the instructor on a rotating basis.

3.4   Gender studies

Women, Gender, Difference is a 3.0-unit, one-term course in the Department of Gender Studies. It serves as the first-year gateway course for concentrations in Gender Studies, and as an elective course for students in other concentrations. The traditional course required each student to attend one 2-hour lecture per week in a single large section of 275 students, taught by the instructor of the course. Each week, each student also attended one one-hour teaching assistant-led tutorial. These tutorials were divided into several sections consisting of 25 students each.

In the 2012/13 academic year, the course instructor began the initial phase of converting the course to a flipped format. In addition to completing work online and through readings, the blended course required each student to attend one hour-long lecture per week as well as one hour-long, facilitated active-learning lab per week. Lectures were delivered by the instructor in a single large section of 300 students, while group learning labs were facilitated by graduate teaching assistants. Group learning labs consisted of 25 students and within these labs students worked on specific tasks in groups of 5.

4   Impact on student engagement

The Course Redesign Project is designed to enhance student engagement and improve student learning in large, introductory courses. To examine the impact of adopting a blended model on student engagement, data was collected in the last offering of the traditional format and in the initial offering of the blended format for each participating course. Toward the end of each semester, all students in a course were invited to complete a paper-based version of the Student Class-Level Survey of Student Engagement (Student CLASSE). Ouimet and Smallwood (2005) describe the Student CLASSE as an engagement survey that measures student engagement at the course level. The 40-item Student CLASSE consists of five sections: engagement activities, cognitive skills, other educational practices, class atmosphere, and demographics. The engagement activities section is made up of 19 items derived from the National Survey of Student Engagement (NSSE), the cognitive skills section consists of a set of five items related to Bloom's Taxonomy, and finally the other educational practices and class atmosphere sections include items developed to examine students' study habits and study styles (Ouimet and Smallwood, 2005).

To examine the impact of course redesign on student engagement and learning, the main focus of the data analysis has been on the 19 items in the engagement activities section of the Student CLASSE and the five items that make up the cognitive or higher order thinking skills section. The 19 engagement activities items were organized into six scalelets based on results of principal components analysis with promax (oblique) rotation.

Brenda Ravenscroft and Ulemu Luhanga

According to Pike (2006, p 552) scalelets consist of sets of survey questions related to specific aspects of students' educational experiences. The six scalelets were labelled: active learning during class, active learning outside class, collaborative learning, course challenge, student-faculty interactions, and writing skills. Examples of items within each scalelet are shown in Table 1, together with a sample item for the higher order thinking skills subscale.

Table 1: Scalelets and sample items

Scalelet	Sample item
1. Active learning during class	Asked questions during class
2. Active learning outside class	Participated in a community-based project
3. Collaborative learning	Worked with classmates outside class
4. Course challenge	Worked harder than you expected
5. Student-faculty interactions	Discussed grades/assignment with instructor
6. Writing skills	Prepared two or more drafts of a paper
7. Higher order thinking skills	How much coursework involved **applying** theories or concepts to practical problems

Scalelet scores were obtaining by calculating the average score for items that made up a scalelet. Each item on the Student CLASSE is on a 4-point scale, as a result, scalelet scores could range from 1 (indicating no engagement) to 4 (high levels of engagement). These scalelets were therefore used to answer the question: are students in flipped formats engaged in their learning differently than those in the traditional formats?

To answer this question, independent sample T-tests were conducted to determine whether there were statistically significant differences between scalelet scores for students in flipped formats versus those in traditional formats. In each of the four courses, baseline data were collected at the end of the last traditional offering of the course (the 2010/11 academic year for the Psychology course, 2011/12 for the other three courses), with data being collected for the first offering of the flipped format at the end of the subsequent academic years. Within the Psychology course, a sample of 549 out of 1,454 (37.8%) students provided baseline data while a sample of 1,417 out of 1,742 (81.3%) students provided data for the first flipped model offering. Similarly, in Sociology, baseline data was provided by a sample of 201 out of 742 (28%) students while a sample of 455 out of 771

(59%) students provided data for the first offering of the flipped version. Within the Classics course, a sample of 107 out of 409 (26%) students provided baseline data while a sample of 489 out of 560 (87%) students provided data for the course's first flipped offering. Finally, within the Gender Studies course, baseline data was provided by a sample of 118 out of 273 (43%) students while a sample of 140 out of 298 (47%) students provided data for the first offering of the flipped version of the course.

4.1   Engagement and employability skills

Initially, two scalelets were of particular interest to the Course Redesign Project: active learning during class and student-faculty interactions. Enhancements in both aspects were confirmed when the results showed statistically significant ($p < 0.05$) average engagement scores in active learning during class and student-faculty interactions in the majority of the courses. The engagement data also offer valuable insight into the skills that are associated with employability. Specifically, two scalelets connect to fundamental skills that have been identified as critical to employment: collaborative learning is linked to team work, while writing skills are central to communication. In addition, higher order thinking skills speak directly to the problem-solving and critical-thinking skills sought after by employers. It is instructive to examine the results for these three scalelets to see the effect of course format on learning associated with employability skills.

Results of independent sample T-tests for three scalelets—collaborative learning, writing skills and higher order thinking skills—are presented in Tables 2, 3, 4, and 5 for the Psychology, Sociology, Classics, and Gender Studies courses respectively. Across all four courses average scalelet scores were higher in the flipped learning format than in the traditional format, with one exception (the higher order thinking skills subscale for Gender Studies, which showed a lower average score in the flipped format). Supporting student perceptions of greater engagement in the flipped formats, in three of the four courses statistically significant ($p < 0.05$) differences were found for the collaborative learning scalelet (Psychology, Sociology, Gender Studies). In terms of writing skills in the Psychology, Sociology and Classics courses, greater engagement in the flipped formats was also evident and statistically significant ($p < 0.05$). Both the Psychology and Classics courses indicated statistically significant ($p < 0.05$) improvements in higher order thinking skills in the flipped formats, although students re-

Brenda Ravenscroft and Ulemu Luhanga

ported lower average scores in the Gender Studies course (also statistically significant at p < 0.05). Overall, however, the flipped formats adopted by each course were perceived to promote greater student engagement than the traditional learning formats.

Table 2: Results for psychology course

Scalelet		Sample size	Average score	Standard deviation
Collaborative learning	Traditional	510	1.706	.700
	Flipped	1,393	**1.924***	.608
Writing skills	Traditional	508	1.159	.401
	Flipped	1,389	**1.979***	.676
Higher order thinking skills	Traditional	507	2.482	.851
	Flipped	1.380	**2.694***	.717

statistically significant difference found between formats using alpha = 0.05

Table 3: Results for sociology course

Scalelet		Sample size	Average score	Standard deviation
Collaborative learning	Traditional	187	1.828	.571
	Flipped	455	**2.062***	.581
Writing skills	Traditional	186	2.4310	.557
	Flipped	455	**2.628***	.680
Higher order thinking skills	Traditional	184	2.520	.709
	Flipped	452	**2.581**	.709

statistically significant difference found between formats using alpha = 0.05

41

Table 4: Results for classics course

Scalelet		Sample size	Average score	Standard deviation
Collaborative learning	Traditional	107	1.937	.763
	Flipped	486	**2.038**	.670
Writing skills	Traditional	107	1.237	.557
	Flipped	489	**2.137***	.680
Higher order thinking skills	Traditional	101	2.047	.765
	Flipped	476	**2.278***	.735

statistically significant difference found between formats using alpha = 0.05

Table 5: Results for gender studies course

Scalelet		Sample size	Average score	Standard deviation
Collaborative learning	Traditional	118	1.715	.469
	Flipped	119	**1.887***	.480
Writing skills	Traditional	118	2.565	.574
	Flipped	125	2.589	.609
Higher order thinking skills	Traditional	117	2.964	. 639
	Flipped	108	**2.690***	.705

statistically significant difference found between formats using alpha = 0.05

5 Discussion

The improvements in average engagement scores in the collaborative learning scalelet in the Psychology, Sociology and Gender Studies courses are likely attributable to the deliberate inclusion of structured group activities in the weekly learning labs. Prior to being developed into blended formats, all three courses were comprised primarily of lectures. Tutorials were treated as optional and were usually structured in a conventional way with teaching assistants reviewing the week's materials and answering student questions. The redesign process focuses on the development of small group activities, where students, working in groups of 5 – 8, are expected to complete work before class, to collaborate during the activity, and occasionally, to assess their peers. Activities are documented in course manuals to ensure consistency between different groups, and teaching assistants play the role of facilitators rather than instructors. In the case of the Psychology course, students are assigned to work in the same groups for the duration of the course to promote accountability and increase group cohesion. Collaborative group assignments require students to work through concepts with their peers and provide opportunities for the application and extension of concepts. In one of the activities, students participate in a simulation, combine their individual data, and write a brief group lab report applying the scientific method. In the process of these collaborative activities, students learn how to interact with a group of diverse individuals, how to manage conflict, and how to contribute to a team by sharing information, all skills that map onto those seen as desirable for employability.

Developing students' writing capabilities, one of the key elements in a set of communication skills, is often seen as particularly challenging in courses with high enrolments (Hobson and Shafermeyer, 1994). The statistically significant improvements in average engagement scores in the writing skills scalelet in the Psychology, Sociology and Classics courses suggests that the flipped format may provide a way to address this challenge. The shift away from the lecture as the primary focus of the course means that less time is occupied by the transmission of information, and more time can be spent on active learning components. For example, the blended Sociology course includes a staged writing assignment, developed in collaboration with the university library and the writing centre. Students are guided through the process of recognizing and using high quality data sources and undergo iterative writing practice. Peer evaluation, which takes place in the small group setting, helps students to develop stronger thesis statements and persuasive arguments for their written assignments, resulting in an overall higher quality final product.

While improvements in average engagement scores for the higher order thinking subscale in the flipped versions of Psychology and Classics are encouraging, the statistically significant decrease in the Gender Studies course raises questions and suggests further review of the course design is needed. One factor that may have played a role is staffing: the course underwent an unexpected change of instructor very late in the development process, when the experienced instructor was replaced by someone who had never taught the course before.

In conclusion, focusing innovation on the development of flipped formats for large introductory courses has yielded promising preliminary results showing improvements in aspects such as collaborative learning, writing skills and higher order thinking skills. While it is premature to draw conclusions about longer term effects, these initial positive results suggest that the Course Redesign Project—which now includes over 8,000 enrolments—could have a significant impact, not only by improving the student learning experience, but also by equipping students with the skills needed for future employment.

References

Ambrose, S.A., Bridges, M.W., DiPietro, M., Lovett, M.C., Norman, M.K. and Mayer R.E. (2010) How Learning Works: Seven Research-Based Principles for Smart Teaching, Jossey-Bass, San Francisco.

Carle, A C, Jaffee, D, and Miller, D (2009) "Engaging College Science Students and Changing Academic Achievement with Technology: A Quasi-Experimental Preliminary Investigation", Computers & Education, Vol 52, No. 2, pp 376–380.

Conference Board of Canada (2014) Employability Skills, available from: http://www.conferenceboard.ca/topics/education/learning-tools/employability-skills.aspx.

Garrison, D. and Vaughan, N. (2008) Blended Learning in Higher Education: Framework, Principles, and Guidelines, John Wiley & Sons, San Francisco, CA.

Hobson, E. and Schafermeyer, K. (1994) "Writing and Critical Thinking: Writing-to-Learn in Large Classes", American Journal of Pharmaceutical Education, Vol 58, No. 4, pp 423–427.

Mayer, R.E. (2008) Learning and instruction, Pearson/Merrill Prentice-Hall, Upper Saddle River, NJ.

Means, B., Toyama, Y., Murphy, R., Bakia, M. and Jones, K. (2010) Evaluation of Evidence-Based Practices in Online Learning: A Meta-Analysis and Review of Online Learning, Washington: US Department of Education, Office of Planning, Evaluation, and Policy Development.

Brenda Ravenscroft and Ulemu Luhanga

Michael, J. (2006) "Where's the Evidence that Active Learning Works"? Advances in Physiology Education, Vol 30, pp 159–167.

Middendorf, J. and Kalish, A. (1996) The 'Change Up' in Lectures", The National Teaching and Learning Forum, Vol 5, No. 2, pp 1–7.

Minhas, P.S., Ghosh, A. and Swanzy, I. (2012) "The Effects of Passive and Active Learning on Student Preference and Performance in an Undergraduate Basic Science Course", Anatomical Sciences Education, Vol 5, pp 200–207.

Ministry of Training, Universities and Colleges (2009) Essential Employability Skills, available from: http://www.tcu.gov.on.ca/pepg/audiences/colleges/progstan/essential.html.

Ouimet, J.A. and Smallwood, R.A. (2005) "CLASSE — The Class-Level Survey of Student Engagement", Assessment Update, Vol 17, pp 13–16.

Pike, G.R. (2006) "The Convergent and Discriminant Validity of NSSE Scalelet Scores", Journal of College Student Development, Vol 47, pp 550–563.

Twigg, C.A. (2000) "Course-Readiness Criteria: Identifying Targets of Opportunity for Large-Scale Redesign", Educause Review, Vol 35, No. 3, pp 41–49.

Vaughan, N.D. (2007) "Perspectives on Blended Learning in Higher Education", International Journal on E-learning, Vol 6, No. 1, pp 81–94.

Vaughan, N.D. (2010) "A Blended Community of Inquiry Approach: Linking Student Engagement and Course Redesign", The Internet and Higher Education, Vol 13, Nos. 1-2, pp 60–65.

Wirth, K.R. (2007) "Teaching for Deeper Understanding and Lifelong Learning", Elements, Vol 2, pp 107–111.

A Lecturer's Perception of the Adoption of the Inverted Classroom or Flipped Method of Curriculum Delivery in a Hydrology Course, in a Resource Poor University of Technology

Eunice Ivala, Anton Thiart and Daniela Gachago
Cape Peninsula University of Technology, Cape Town, South Africa
Originally published in the Proceedings of ICEL 2013

Editorial commentary

Ivala, Thiart & Gachado take a perspective that differs from the previous chapter: they examine the flipped method from the teacher's perspective. Their experience suggest that although it is time consuming (preparation, video shooting, class activities), this method proved to be useful for promoting deep learning. More-over, it enhanced teacher satisfaction in terms of the attempt to, a"...bring back some excitement in teaching." This is an important statement, and the authors suggest that, ...transmissive models of teaching ..."have had their time". I personally hear more and more from teachers who want to change. They feel that something is not right, that students expect something different. Generation Y or Z students habitually consume short and often high quality videos, play 3D games with complex scenarios. It is not surprising that they no longer wish to sit in lectures for hours listening to a text-heavy presentation about a topic they might not interested in. What would you do if you were in their shoes? Take your smart-phone/laptop and type, probably...and that's what they do.

Eunice Ivala, Anton Thiart and Daniela Gachago

I don't claim learning should always be easy access on demand. On the contrary, learning is a hard and sometimes a painful process of deconstruction/construction. However the format of 1 hour – 3 hour lectures is dead and this is part of the reason that the flipped model is successful. The concept is not new, however. Active learning in class has always been implemented. Nonetheless video capture technology has made it much easier to do, giving impetus to the phenomenon.

Abstract: The core business of any higher education institution (HEI) is to provide quality learning to its students by facilitating deep learning. More often than not, this goal is not fully achieved in most HEIs globally. This is in part due to over-reliance on the lecture method of delivering instruction, a method which is not a particularly effective medium for promoting deep learning. The delivery of instruction in Civil Engineering at a University of Technology, South Africa, is predominantly via the lecture method. As a result, an alternative method of delivering curriculum in this field maybe needed in order to improve student learning. Informed by a modified technology acceptance model, this paper presents a lecturer's perceptions on the adoption and benefits of the inverted classroom method (ICM) of delivering instruction in a hydrology course, in the Civil Engineering field. A qualitative approach of collecting data was used and the data consisted of recordings of an in-depth interview with the lecturer and a workshop facilitated by the lecturer to introduce the ICM to 11 lecturers from various disciplines in the university. Data analysis was done deductively whereby relevant data were mapped to the constructs given in the conceptual framework. Some key findings were that the lecturer implemented the ICM due to his self-efficacy, technological self-efficacy and perceived usefulness of the ICM of curriculum delivery. The study also highlights the challenges experienced in, and effective ways of implementation, of the ICM of curriculum delivery at the university. Findings of this study will give insights and ideas on the adoption and benefits of the ICM of curriculum delivery in an engineering field at the university and also in other resource-poor contexts, particularly in the African continent, where there is limited research and use of the ICM for instruction.

Keywords: inverted classroom or flipped method of curriculum delivery, technology acceptance model, the lecture method of curriculum delivery, teacher self-efficacy, technological self-efficacy

47

1   Introduction

The main business of any higher education institution (HEI) is to provide quality learning to its students, which can be facilitated by deep learning. More often than not, this goal is not fully achieved in most HEIs globally. This is in part due to over-reliance on the lecture method of delivering instruction, a method which is not a particularly effective medium for promoting deep learning (Johnson et al. 1991; Bates & Galloway 2012).

Drawing from a modified technology acceptance model (Chigona et al. 2012), this paper presents a lecturer's perceptions on the adoption and benefits of ICM of delivering instruction in a hydrology course, in the Civil Engineering field, at a University of Technology, South Africa. The study was guided by the following questions:

- What factors influenced the lecturer's adoption of the ICM of curriculum delivery?
- What was the lecturer's perceived benefits of implementing ICM to himself and his students?

Some key findings were that the lecturer implemented the ICM due to his self-efficacy, technological self-efficacy and perceived usefulness of the ICM of curriculum delivery.

2   Literature review

Teaching and learning in higher education institutions

Most teaching in higher education is by the lecture method (Bates & Galloway 2012; Koller 2011), with the main emphasis being on coverage of content (Strayer 2007). Johnson et al. (1991) reports on several studies that show lectures are a relatively ineffective way of promoting learning (see also Bates & Galloway 2012). In the lectures, students are introduced to materials or concepts, process the information, solve problems and practice with the course concepts and reach conclusions outside of the class (McDaniel & Caverly 2010; Talbert 2012). In Engineering education, Nguyen and Toto (2009) and Lord and Camacho (2007) report that majority of the classrooms still rely on the lecture model of delivery of course content. While this format has been effective, in practice, we still find significant problems with pacing of instruction and the fact that the most difficult tasks students have to perform generally appear in the work they do

Eunice Ivala, Anton Thiart and Daniela Gachago

outside of class (homework), on their own and separated from the instructor's help (Nguyen & Toto 2009; Talbert 2012).

To improve on student learning, HEIs needs to use pedagogical approaches which promote deep student learning and thus, students' high performance. One of these pedagogical approaches is the 'Inverted classroom method' (ICM) (Gannod et al.2008; Koller 2011), a term coined by a group of economic professors in Miami University (Ohio) (Lage et al. 2000). In the schooling sector, the ICM is often known as the 'flipped classroom, a term coined by Bergmann (2011), a high school Chemistry teacher. The ICM of curriculum delivery uses technology to 'flip' or 'invert' the traditional lecture model (Strayer 2007). The method moves the lecture outside the classroom via technology and moves homework and practice with concepts inside the classroom via learning activities. The primary elements of the ICM are online lecture materials, in audio/video format, that students can access on demand, and a classroom environment that is conducive to working with peers and the lecturer, problem solving and answering questions (Demetry 2010; Gannod et al. 2008; Lage et al. 2000; McDaniel & Caverly 2010; Nguyen & Toto 2009; Strayer 2007). Hence, online materials are used to provide the first introduction to course topics and classroom time is used to process the information and solve problems. According to Lage at el. (2000), the inverted classroom environment is not a new idea and Gardner (2012:2) argues that, "the modern version of inverted class, which is characterized by online videos, is already over a decade old". However, the method is new to many faculty and in recent times, has received increased attention.

An advantage of the ICM are the out-of-class activities, which include students watching online videos introducing course concepts, showing examples, giving quizzes or exercises and modeling problem solving process (Doering & Mu 2010; Talbert 2012). By using videos this way, students who would have found the lecture pace slow are able to work quickly through material that they already know and delve into more interesting and challenging problems (Koller 2011). Students who would have struggled with concepts can access the course materials when they are ready to learn, and at anytime of the day and are able to rewind and watch tricky segments many times (Gannod et al.2008; Gardner 2012; Strayer 2007). Stu-

49

dents can also pause and reflect on the lecture materials when needed (Talbert 2012).

By watching the videos out of class, students arrive in class prepared to practice the ideas to which they've already been exposed. An assignment over the material is given and student work in groups. The students are involved in active and peer learning, while the lecturer walks around, observing their work and offering appropriate assistance. Students who struggle with the concepts benefit from the instructors time, time that the instructor spends identifying the particular and individual sources of a student's confusion, hence promoting personalized instruction. The faster students may also serve as peer mentors (Gannod et al. 2008; Koller 2012; McDaniel & Caverly 2010; Strayer 2007) for the other students in the class, this would mean the slower students have more help available to learn the concepts. The faster students might achieve the deeper understanding that comes from explaining a concept to someone else. This might also mitigate the risk in self-paced learning where a student quickly crams through material, but isn't engaged with it for a long enough time for long-term retention.

The ICM is criticized for assuming that every student has access to technology (computer, smartphone or tablet) and Internet connectivity (Gardner 2012), an unrealistic expectation especially in developing countries, like South Africa. For the method to work well for instructional delivery, majority of the students must engage with the online materials before class, a scenario that is highly unlikely without developing an enforcement mechanism. Furthermore, developing inverted classroom materials is labour intensive and time consuming (Bates & Galloway 2012; Talbert 2012), for lecturers who are expected to teach as well as do research. However, ICM is still useful despite the criticisms.

Even with this potential to promote effective learning, there are few research studies that specifically investigate the ICM globally (Strayer 2007), and particularly in Africa.This paper presents a lecturer's perceptions on the adoption and benefits of ICM of delivering instruction in a hydrology course, in the civil Engineering field, at a University of Technology, South Africa.

3   Course details

The hydrology course is a third year module within the Water Engineering subject 3 and contributes 50% of marks towards the subject. The water Engineering 3 subject contributes towards the attainment of a national diploma in Civil Engineering. It is a compulsory one semester course taught in the second semester, with two one- hour lectures per week. The course is aimed at imparting the principles and practices of engineering hydrology through the use of examples and calculations. The lecture method of curriculum delivery is used to teach course content, supplemented by student interaction with information through home work, lab session, project and discussions out of class to make meaning of the course content. The course was co-taught by two lecturers.

Inverted classroom method was not implemented in the delivery of the entire course but on selected topics of the course. The selected topics were: introduction to hydrology; meteorological data; evaporation and transpiration; and infiltration and percolation. The lecturer implemented the ICM by providing basic materials on course content to students via online videos (using a shared drive on the institutional intranet for long videos and Dropbox for short videos as access systems), short documents on the course website and continuously encouraging the students to engage with the materials through a closed Facebook group. Links from Dropbox were also posted in the Facebook group. Students were supposed to engage with the online materials at home in preparation for the class. In class, students worked in groups with more complex questions on the course content, with the lecturer assisting and guiding them when needed and students helping each other.

4   Theoretical framework

The paper draws on a modified technology acceptance model (TAM) (Chigona et al. 2012), to investigate and understand a lecturer's perceptions on the adoption and benefits of ICM of delivering instruction in a hydrology course, in the Civil Engineering field. Although this model's focus is on technology acceptance, we felt that it would be suitable for understanding the adoption of ICM since the method relies heavily on technology. The adapted TAM framework (see figure 1) was developed by integrating two constructs (technological self-efficacy and teacher self efficacy) onto Davis'

(1989) original model (see figure 2), which stipulates that individuals accept and use a new technology if they perceive it to be useful and easy to use which both determine an individual's intention to use of the innovation. According to McDonald and Siegall (1992), technological self-efficacy is "the belief in one's ability to successfully perform a technologically sophisticated new task".

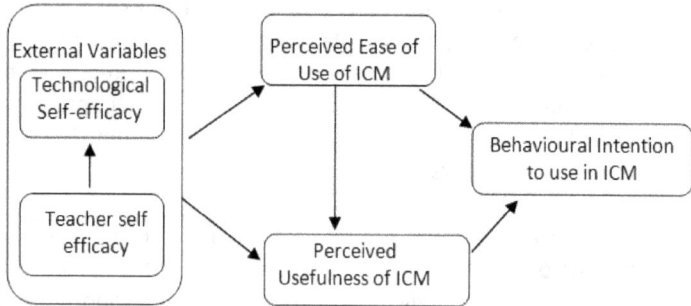

Figure 1: Conceptual framework adapted from Davis' original TAM Model (Chigona et al. 2012)

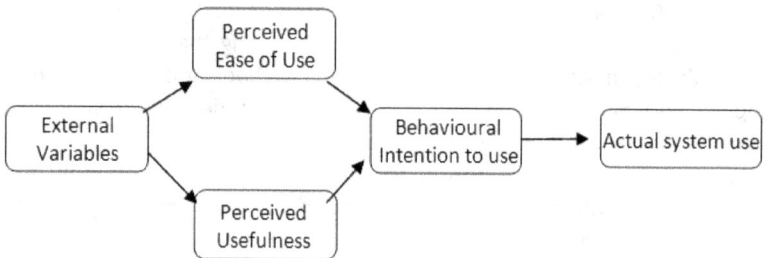

Figure 2: Technology acceptance model (Davis 1989)

An example of technological self-efficacy is an individual's perception of his or her ability to use computers in the accomplishment of a task rather than reflecting a simple component skill (Compeau & Higgins 1995). Research show that technological self-efficacy influences perceived usefulness and perceived ease of use of a technology (Chigona et al. 2012; Skoretz 2011). On the other hand, teacher's efficacy is defined as the teacher's "judgment of his or her capabilities to bring about desired outcomes of student engagement and learning, even among those students who may be difficult or unmotivated" (Tscannen-Moran & Hoy 2001:1).

Perceived usefulness is "the degree to which a person believes that using a particular system would enhance his or her job performance" (Davis 1989), while perceived ease-of-use is "the degree to which a person believes that using a particular system would be free from effort" (Davis 1989).

5 Methodology

A qualitative approach was employed in this study with an aim of understanding a lecturer's perceptions on the adoption and benefits of ICM of delivering instruction in a hydrology course, in the Civil Engineering field. This approach was suitable for the study because of its strength in investigating experiences as they are 'lived' or 'felt' or 'undergone' by the participants (Sherman & Webb 1988).

5.1 Context and participants

The main participant in this study is an Engineering lecturer (the first lecturer to use ICM of curriculum delivery at the university), who implemented the ICM of curriculum delivery in a hydrology class in 2012 and offered a training workshop to 11 lecturers on ICM in November 2012. Thus, purposive sampling was used (Neuman 1997). He was chosen because he had rich information gained through practice (Patton 1990) and was thought to be likely to reflect on the complexity of implementing the ICM in a resource–poor institution like this university.

5.2 Data collection

A qualitative approach of collecting data was used. Data consisted of recordings of an in-depth interview with the lecturer and a workshop facilitated by the lecturer to introduce the ICM to 11 lecturers from various disciplines in the university.

5.3 Data analysis

Data was analysed using the adapted TAM Framework constructs. The constructs were: technological self-efficacy; teacher self efficacy; perceived usefulness of the ICM; and perceived ease of use of the ICM (see figure 2). Analysis was done deductively whereby relevant data were mapped to the constructs given in the conceptual framework. The researchers in this study acknowledge that findings of this study are not generalisable, but offer valuable insights, which others interested in the implementation of the ICM of curriculum delivery could draw from.

Consent to participate in the study was sought and the purpose of the study was explained to the lecturer. Interview and workshop transcripts were available for the lecturer to scrutinize. Anonymity and confidentiality was adhered to as promised to the lecturer. Ethical clearance was given by the institutional ethics committee.

6 Results and discussion

The paper reports on a lecturer's perceptions on the adoption and benefits ICM of delivering instruction in a hydrology course, in the civil Engineering field, at University of Technology, South Africa. Findings and discussion are presented under the following categories.

- Technological self-efficacy
- Teacher self efficacy
- Perceived usefulness of the ICM
- Perceived ease of use of the ICM

6.1 Technological self-efficacy

According to Compeau & Higgins (1995), an example of technological self-efficacy is an individual's perception of his or her ability to use computers in the accomplishment of a task rather than reflecting a simple component skill. Inverted classroom method relies heavily on technology, but most faculty at this university, like elsewhere, have not learned their subject content with these technologies and hence do not have essential experiences in learning with these technologies nor have they been prepared to teach their content with these new and emerging technologies (Niess 2011). However, the lecturer in this study implemented ICM partly because he possessed technological self-efficacy:

> *...although I've studied Engineering I also come from a very strong IT background ...I did three year Software Diploma and I've always been interested in technology. I think I'm not scared of technology. I*

find it sometimes a stumbling block for lecturers to get because they are a little bit scared of technology and ...for me it is second nature.

From the above results, it can be inferred that lecturers' technological self-efficacy influence their decisions to adopt ICM of curriculum delivery, due to the methods reliance on technology for delivering course materials outside the classroom (Strayer 2007). Technological self-efficacy is needed in order for a lecturer to be able to source or develop the online materials.

6.2   Teacher self efficacy

The ICM of curriculum delivery, uses technology to 'flip' or 'invert' the traditional lecture model (Strayer 2007) by moving the lecture outside the classroom via technology and homework and practice with concepts inside the classroom via learning activities. To change from delivering instruction using the lecture method, a method which dominates most teaching in HE globally (Bates & Galloway 2012; Koller 2011), the lecturers need to have self-efficacy (lecturers' "judgment of his or her capabilities to bring about the desired outcomes of students engagement and learning" (Tscannen-Moran & Hoy 2001:1). Lecturers' who have positive self-efficacy will feel confident to include new pedagogical approaches in their classroom. In this study, the lecturer seemed confident enough to teach using the ICM. The lecturer's self-efficacy to teach with ICM is demonstrated in the following quotes:

...I had a particular problem this year that they gave me ...two hour slots after lunch two days, on consecutive days. So the students arrived tired, struggled to concentrate... So I thought, you know, I cannot use normal techniques here, it's not going to work, you know because they'll fall asleep ... Now if I can get them involved, I can hear them talking and engaging, I feel that's a great way of stimulating conversation and learning more...

...I've lectured a lot of subjects over many years and it does get boring doing the same thing over and over and it's probably my biggest motivation ...I'm looking for things that makes it not only interesting for the student but start making it interesting for me because it's my job ... Making things exciting but it's nice and that's why some

lecturers are also actually buying in on it because it brings back some excitement in their teaching ...

The above findings show that this lecturer had very high levels of self-efficacy as he was able to reflect on his own teaching methods (lecture method) and the context of teaching (lecture time slots at lunch time when students are tired) and how it impacted on students learning (students not concentrating). He was also able to come up with ways of changing his teaching and student learning, which included the decision to adopt the ICM in order to be able to actively engage students in learning. He also adopted the method to make his work more enjoyable and exciting. The lecturer's self–efficacy was also shown by the fact that he was confident enough to facilitate a staff training workshop on the ICM at the university.

6.3   Perceived usefulness of the ICM

It is commonsense that many faculty would adopt a new pedagogical approach when the approach is perceived to help improve the teaching and learning process. According to Davis (1989) perceived usefulness is the degree to which a person believes that using a particular system would enhance his or her job. The lecturer in this study believed that the ICM of curriculum delivery was useful for facilitating deep learning and enhancing his job, as evidenced in the following quotes:

> *...the things I did right was the whole idea of giving the material beforehand, basic material and then coming to class and then carry on with a little bit more advanced examples... questions that require cognitive engagement, when I'm there to prompt them and help them and they help each other obviously. They help each other actually a lot. Sometimes they don't even want the lecturer to give them help... what happens in normal classrooms is the lecturer stands up and ...does basic examples and then he tells students' to go back do homework and the homework is then more advanced...*

> *... it [ICM] enriched my job because I'm unfortunately in the situation that I will probably be stuck as a lecturer ... till I retire. So I have to make my life interesting. I have to enrich my own life and I have to use new methods. And it definitely did ... I'm getting some expo-*

Eunice Ivala, Anton Thiart and Daniela Gachago

sure, meeting some new people...and I'm making new contacts all the time now...

6.4 Perceived ease of use of the ICM

The perceived ease–of-use of an innovation is "the degree to which a person believes that using a particular system would be free from effort" (Davis 1989). The way lecturers perceive how easy the ICM is to use in the classroom influence their decision to adopt the method for their teaching or not. In this study, the lecturer indicated that the method was useful for enhancing deep student learning and his job, but expressed that the method was not ease to use because it was labour intensive and time consuming to make the online materials and that one needed to motivate students to ensure that they engaged with course materials at home.

I don't think it's easy because it takes a lot of preparation... you have to prepare new material where you could have just stuck with the old, ... it takes time to make little videos and editing it. ...to actually shoot the video it takes probably four/five times as long to edit it...

I believe that this inverted classroom needs to go hand in hand with a good communication tool because if you want to give students stuff to do outside the classroom there needs to be constant communication... I think a major problem would be just to let the student be and when he comes to class again then he says well I didn't understand what I was supposed to do or whatever.... I set up Facebook ...for the subject and I had all 50 students actually in the group and it was a closed group... we had constant questions from students, posting of things that's happening, go look on the shared drive for this thing and do that. So the instructions didn't only take place in the classroom, the communication went right through the week.

These results are similar to findings by Bates and Galloway (2012) and Talbert (2012). According to the lecturer, a mind shift on how one teaches is needed to embrace the ICM and constant communication with students is required to ensure that students engage with course materials outside the classroom. The lecturer also reported that at the university it was not ease to use the ICM because of contextual and social issues, as he explained in the following quotes:

> *...let's say two lecturers lecture the same subject we have to agree on the assessment. Now this deeper learning that took place might not be assessed because we're back to the old way of let's say we taught in class and we have to assess those basic things. So maybe if a paper was set with more higher level questions it would have come out more clearly. But I must say my class did way better than the other group but I can't say it was because of the inverted...*

> *...I don't know about other places but you can come and look at our classrooms. They're terrible ...I want to show a little video of something ... using a data projector, I don't have sound, then you could hardly see because there's no way I can make the classroom a bit darker. It's very noisy and it's uncomfortable...*
> *... what is happening because our facilities are so poor, if I have to go to class and use technology there, I bought myself a trolley. In the trolley I put my laptop, data projector, my two speakers, my extension cord... Now I trolley this to the classroom...tea time I would go fifteen minutes before the time ...and set up my things. And then of course at lunchtime when we stop I have to take down all this lot again – put it in my trolley and off I go back. Now that in itself is really a big stumbling block for anyone who wants to implement this because it's really too much hassle.*

The above findings show that co-teaching a course, poor classroom conditions, and lack of technology and technical support in the use of technology in teaching and learning may hinder lecturers' use of the ICM at the university. The provision of good teaching facilities and technical support in the use of technology would make lecturers find the ICM easy to use.

7 Conclusion

Findings of the study show that the lecturer perceived the use of the ICM of curriculum delivery significant for promoting deep learning and enhancing job satisfaction. Through this method, the lecturer managed to create a learning environment which encouraged student participation in class (both for slow and high aptitude students); independent learning; high students-student interaction with the course content; student-contents interaction and student-lecturer interaction, characteristics of teaching and learning which promote deep learning (Anderson 2003). Additionally, results indicate that lecturers' adoption of the ICM is to some extent affected by lecturers' technological self-efficacy coupled with teacher self efficacy, as the lecturer in this study adopted the method partly due to his self efficacy and technological self-efficacy. Because of the labor intensity and time needed to produce online materials, and the contextual and social issues at the university, the lecturer perceived the adoption of the ICM not easy.

Findings of the study also demonstrated that it is important for lecturers to try innovative pedagogical approaches because it demonstrates to the students that the lecturers are trying to help them learn, which may improve their motivation.

...I think students are becoming more and more technology savvy...If you look at the response of students [on the use of ICM] they're actually fine with you trying these type of things and they do enjoy it because that's what they are using everyday [technology]
We are also convinced that an institution that aspires to greatness and innovation has to be open to support a wide variety of pedagogical approaches, of which ICM is one.

Further in-depth research will be done to examine students' perceptions on the use of the ICM for their instruction in this course.

References

Anderson, T. (2003). "Getting the mix right: an updated and theoretical rationale for interaction", Vol.4, No. 2. [online] http://www.irrodl.org/index.php/irrodl/article/view/149

Bates, S. and Galloway, R. (2012). "The inverted classroom in a large enrolment introductory physics course: a case study", Higher Education Academy, [online], http://www.heacademy.ac.uk/assets/documents/stem-conference/PhysicalSciences/Simon_Bates_Ross_Galloway.pdf

Bergmann, B. (2011). "The history of the flipped class: how the flipped class was born (Web log post)", [Online]http://www.blendedclassroom.blogpost.com/

Chigona, A., Condy, J., Gachago, D. and Ivala, E. (2012). "Examining pre-service teachers' perceptions on uptake of digital storytelling for classroom use", In

Proceedings of World Conference on E-Learning in Corporate, Government, Healthcare, and Higher Education 2012 (pp. 1621-1628). Chesapeake, VA: AACE. [Online] http://www.editlib.org/p/41839

Compeau, D.R. and Higgins, C.A. (1995). "Computer self-efficacy: development of a measure and initial tests", MIS Quarterly , Vol. 19 , No. 2, 189-211

Davis, F.E. (1989). "Perceived usefulness, perceived ease of use, and user acceptance of information Technology", MIS Quarterly, Vol., 13, No. 3, 319-340

Demetry , C. (2010). "Work in progress-an innovation merging "classroom Flip" and team-based learning", 40 th ASEE/IEEE Frontiers in Education Conference, Washington, DC, October 27-30

Doering, E. and Mu, X. (2010). " CLEO: circuit learned by example online", [Online] http://www.rose_hulman.edu/cleo

Gannod, G. C., Burge, J.E., and Helmick, M.T. (2008). "Using the inverted classroom to teach software engineering," In proceedings of the 30 th International Conference on Software Engineering (Liepzing, Germany, ACM, New York, NY-777-786, May 10-18, DOI, [Online] http://doi.acm.org/10.1145/1368088.1368198

Gardner, J. G. (2012). "The inverted agricultural economics classroom: A new way to teach? A new way to learn?", Selected paper prepared for presentation at the Agriculture and Applied Economics Association's 2012 AAEA Annual meeting, Seatle, Washington, August 12-14

Johnson, D. W., Johnson, R. T. and Smith, K. A. (1991). Cooperative learning: increased college faculty instructional productivity, ASHE-ERIC Higher education Report No. 4, The George Washington University, School of Education and Human Development, Washington , D. C

Koller, D. (2011). "Death knell for the lecture: Technology as a passport to personalized education", The New York Times, Reprints.

Lage, M., Platt, G., and Treglia, M. (2000). "Inverting classroom: a gateway to creating an inclusive learning environment", Journal of Economic Education, Vol. 31, No. 1, 30-43

Lord, S. M. and Camacho, M.M. (2007). "Effective teaching practices: preliminary Analysis of Engineering teaching practices", In: Proceedings of the 37 th ASEE/IEEE Frontiers in Education Conference, October

McDaniel, S. and Caverly. D (2010). The community of inquiry model for an inverted developmental math classroom, Journal of Developmental Education, Vol. 34, No. 2.

McDolnald, T., and Siegall, M. (1992). "The effects of technological self-efficacy and job performance, attitudes, and withdraw behaviors", The journal of Psychology, Vol. 126, 465-475

Neuman, W.L. (1997). Social Research Methods: Qualitative and Quantitative approaches, 3rd edn, Allayn and Bacon, Boston

Nguyen, H .M. and Toto, R. (2009). "Flipping the work design in an industrial Engineering course", 39 th ASEE/1EEE Frontiers in Education Conference, San Antonio, TX

Niess, M.L. (2011). "Investigating TPACK: Knowledge growth in teaching with technology", Journal of Educational Computing Research, Vol,. 44, No. 3, 299-317

Patton, M. Q. (1990). Qualitative evaluation and research methods, 2rd edn, Newbury Park, California: sage Publication

Sherman, R. and Webb, R. (Eds.) 1988. Qualitative research in education: Forms and methods, Falmer, Lewes, UK

Skoretz, Y.M. (2011). "A study of the impact of a school-based, job-Embedded professional development program on elementary and middle school teacher efficacy for technology integration. Theses and dissertations, Paper 150". [online] htp://mds.marshall.edu/etd/150

Strayer, J. F. (2007). The effects of the classroom flip on the learning environment: A comparison of learning activity in a traditional classroom and a flip classroom that used an intelligent tutoring system, Presented in partial fulfillment of the requirements' for the degree of Doctor of Philosophy in graduate school of the Ohio State University, USA

Talbert, R. (2012)." Inverted classroom", Colleagues, Vol. 9, No. 1. Article 7, [Online]http://www. scholarworks.gvsu.edu/colleagues/vol9/issue1/7. Accessed 16 January 2013

Tschannen-Moran, M. and Hoy, W.A. (2001). "Teacher efficacy: capturing an elusive construct", Teacher and Teacher Education, Vol., 17, 783-805

A Location-Based Object Identification Algorithm for Augmented Reality in Adaptive Mobile Learning

Qing Tan, William Chang and Kinshuk
School of Computing and Information Systems, Athabasca University,
Athabasca, Canada

Originally published in the Proceedings of ICEL 2014

> ## Editorial commentary
> This chapter offers another point of view on distance learning. It focuses on mobile learning applications using the latest technologies: in this case augmented reality combined with location-based real-life learning objects. In short, the learner's view is augmented with digital information that is tagged with its geographic coordinates. The intention is to use mobile devices to learn in situ, "...at the right time, in the right location, through the right device, providing the right contents to the right learner" (Tan et al, 2011). Tan, Chang and Kinshuk focus on algorithm development, contrary to Power et al. who focus on a serious game of the strategy genre in which gameplay was deeply grounded in collaboration amongst players. The game is both mobile and context aware, with Laval University's campus being transformed into a playing field for teams equipped with mobile devices for an augmented reality competition.
>
> M. Power, S. Daniel, S. Barma and R. Harrap, Playing With Fire: Kindling Learning Through Mobile Gaming. Leading Issues in eLearning Research, Vol. 1, 2011.

Abstract: By superimposing digital learning content on top of the video stream of the mobile device's camera, Augmented Reality (AR) enables learners to interact

62

with real-world context in mobile learning setting. Technically, the AR technology can be considered as consisting of two major aspects: identification of the real-world object and display of computer-generated digital contents related the identified real-world object. In this paper, we will present a location-based object identification algorithm that has been used to identify the location-based learning objects in the 5R adaptive mobile learning system. We will also discuss some issues in using the algorithm. As an example of using this algorithm, an AR mobile application on iPhone will be shown to demonstrate the effectiveness of the location-based object identification algorithm.

Keywords: augmented reality, object identification, location-based adaptive mobile learning

1   Introduction

Augmented Reality (AR) has become a popular display technique in the past few years. It can be defined, as a technique is to display virtual contents superimposed upon real-life objects. On the other hand, the location-based adaptive mobile learning is to provide adaptive learning contents to particular learner according to the learner's location where the real-life context is used as learning objects. In this research, Augmented Reality is considered as an emerging content display technique that can improve and enhance learning content presentation as well as interaction between learners and learning contents associated with location-based real-life learning objects.

It is the essential requirement in order to provide the right content at the right location in the location-based adaptive mobile learning. To apply AR technique for the learning, the major technical challenge is to identify real-life objects (the realities). In order to tackle the technical issue, this paper presents a Location-Based Object Identification Algorithm that we proposed and have implemented in a mobile learning application. The algorithm aims to identify the real-life learning objects (RLO) by matching the tagged location information of the RLOs with the current location and orientation of the mobile device. Furthermore, the algorithm also provides the guidance capability to navigate learner to the right RLO among the nearby RLOs for learning. A real-life learning object is a real-life object used as a location-based learning object in the location-based mobile learning setting.

A location-based adaptive mobile learning application, called Multi-Object Identification Augmented Reality (MOIAR) has been developed to apply AR technique into mobile learning application. It is empowered by the Location-Based Object Identification Algorithm to identify the real-life learning objects in the mobile learning setting. The implementation of the mobile learning application has proven the usability and the practicality of the Location-Based Object Identification Algorithm, To improve the learning content adaptability, the MOIAR also utilizes the 5R adaptive mechanism, which not only provides adaptive learning contents but also assists real-life learning object identification (Chang & Tan & Fang, 2010). The 5R adaptation concept for location-based mobile learning is stated as: at the right time, in the right location, through the right device, providing the right contents to the right learner (Tan, et al, 2011).

In this paper, we will review the related work following by this section. Then in section 3 we will present the Location-based Object Identification Algorithm in detail. In section 4, we will give a location-based mobile learning scenario study where the MOIAR application is used at the Legislative Assembly of Alberta as a real-life learning object to show usability and effectiveness of the algorithm. Finally this paper will be concluded with discussion of future works.

2   Related work

In Augmented Reality, markers are often used in the environment due to their low setting up cost and robustness (Rohs, 2004). However, it is an invasive solution since objects have to be tagged with these codes. On the other hand, emerging tracking systems offer various ways to identify objects in the real world. They range from the well-known Global Positioning System (GPS) to GSM, GPRS and UMTS systems, which enable identification and location of mobile phones within an area of influence (Kalkbrenner & Koppe, 2002). Radio frequency identification systems (RFID) enable non-contact reading of transponders equipped with a worldwide unique identification number (Ferscha, 2002). The emerging wireless sensors network (WSN) systems enable the tracking of mobile devices that are connected to the network through a wireless network card (Ferscha & Beer & Narzt, 2001).

There are many positioning approaches (GPS, WLAN, GSM, transponders, indoor positioning systems, etc.) and orientation identification methods (digital compass, accelerometer, gyros, etc.). They provide all types of tracking information and support different location identification systems. For instance, an active sensing system is able to determine its current position and/or orientation by itself. Built-in A-GPS receiver and digital compass on a mobile phone enable the mobile phone to be able to detect its current position and direction.

3   Location-based object identification algorithm

3.1   The MOIAR overview

AR provides an excellent learning interface in a mobile learning application. The learner's view is augmented with digital information at the correct geographic location, thus providing an intuitive way of presenting such information (Reitmayr & Schmalstieg, 2003). In this paper, the MOIAR application focuses on identifying location-based outdoor real-life learning objects. The MOIAR aims to not only provide the learning contents but also allow learners to interact with the Real-life Learning Objects (RLO) in the simplest and most intuitive way. The MOIAR can also provide learning contents that are adapted and personalized to learners through AR display. In the MOIAR, a mobile AR client application running on a mobile device that is equipped with a built-in A-GPS and a digital compass is used as the tracking device and the learning terminal. The mobile device can continuously track a learner's movement without the need for external references. Sometimes it may be assisted with secondary sensors such as motion sensors (accelerometers) and rotation sensors (gyroscopes). Further, with the implementation of AR and mobile device's location awareness and mobility, the MOIAR has the potential to eliminate some of the learning limitations and disadvantages that exist in the traditional learning. Figure 1 shows the MOIAR application system architecture diagram.

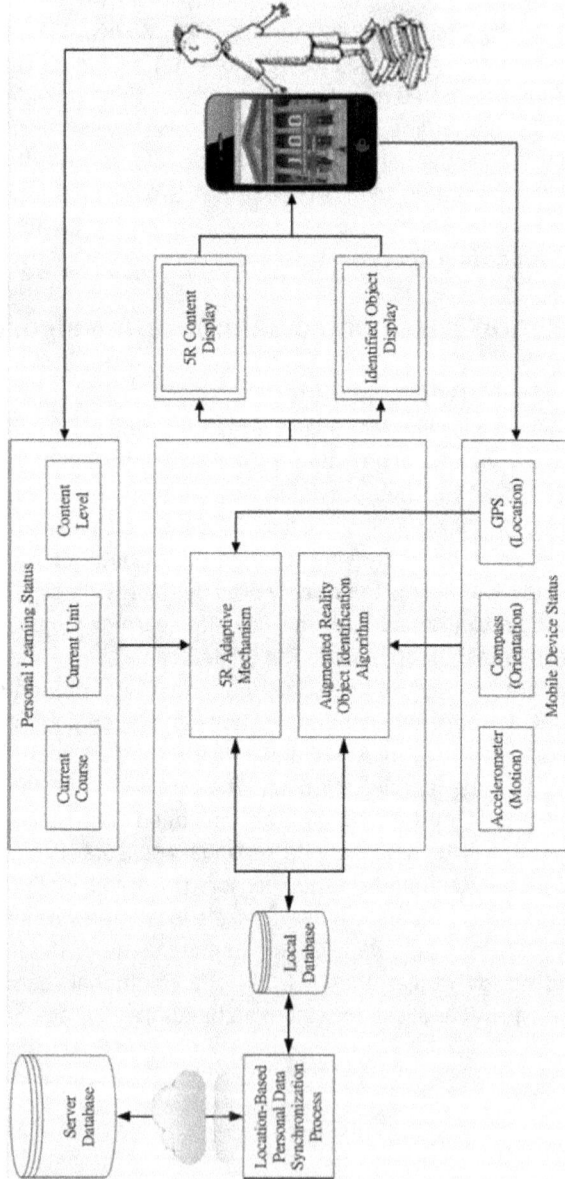

Figure 1: The MOIAR system architecture diagram

66

3.2 Location-based object identification algorithm

In the MOIAR application, AR is used to display digital learning contents related to the real-life learning objects by superimposing upon the video stream of real-life object on the mobile device's screen. This means that the learner carrying the mobile device has to be at a location that is nearby the real-life object, and the learner has to face the mobile device's camera lens towards the real-life object, so that the contents can be seen super-imposed upon the real-life learning object on the screen. To display the right learning contents on the real-life object, the MOIAR has to be able to identify the real-life object i.e. to find which the location-based learning object stored in the database of the mobile learning application match with the real-life object; then the 5R adaptive mechanism will generate right learning contents superimposing on the object.

The idea behind the location-based object identification algorithm for mo-bile Augmented Reality is based on the location-awareness of mobile de-vices and known geographic coordinates of location-based learning objects in the location-based mobile learning environment. The MOIAR mobile application first obtains the current geographic coordinates of the mobile device acquired by the built-in A-GPS sensor. The MOIAR then uses the geographic orientation information to obtain the absolute orientation, which is detected by the built-in digital compass. On the other hand, each location-based learning object predefined and stored in the database has been tagged with its geographic coordinates. When the learner with the mobile device approaching into a pre-configured distance toward a real-life learning object, the MOIAR application will find the object then calcu-lates the relative distance and orientation between the mobile device and the real-life object, which is accomplished by the location-based object identification algorithm.

In fact, in the outdoor learning environment, the locations of real-life ob-jects used as location-based learning objects are known and fixed. When the learner carrying a mobile device is standing nearby a real-life object, it is easy and would make sense for the learner to change his/her current orientation to face the camera lens to the real-life object. Particularly when the object is located in an open space, which means there are no other objects close by or right next to it, the learner can walk around the object as long as he/she is close enough or nearby the object's location, and has mobile device facing the object. Hence, the mobile device's orientation related to the real-life learning object becomes very important.

The location-based object identification algorithm utilizes the concept of the Relative Orientation that will be discussed later in this section. This algorithm also uses two-dimension geographic coordinate information, namely latitude and longitude, to calculate the distance between the learner and the real-life objects. The mobile device's digital compass can get the angle between the mobile camera face and the true north, and then the algorithm can calculate out the angle between mobile camera face and the real-life object. Both of the angles are then used to decide whether the identification tags and the 5R adaptive learning contents should be displayed on the screen or not.

3.2.1 *Distance between mobile device and real-life learning object*
In the MOIAR mobile learning environment, there could be multiple real-life learning objects related to the learner at a particular location. In order to effectively utilize the limited screen space on the mobile device, as well as to provide the the 5R adaptive learning contents, only a certain number of real-life object identification tags and contents should be displayed at the place and time. In the MOIAR application, only objects that match the learner's personal learning profile and status are included into the AR data model as Objects of Interest, and the real-life object identification tags of only those objects may be displayed on the screen at the right location. In fact, in the MOIAR learning environment, learner could be nearby and see several real-life learning objects in different views at one location. However, the learning contents are displayed on the screen only for the real-life learning object that the learner's mobile device's camera lens is pointed to within the pre-configured distance range.

Hence, the relative object identification algorithm is designed to compute the orientation subtended from the learner's current location to each real-life learning object at the location. The MOIAR utilizes two coordinate systems to implement the algorithm. The first coordinate system is the original geographic coordinate systems, known as the Polar coordinate system, which utilizes the latitude, longitude, and the North Pole based orientation. Based on the Polar coordinate system, each real-life learning object's location is indicated as (φ_o, λ_o) as a known parameter, which is predefined and stored in the RLO data model. The learner's current location is indicated as (ϕ_m, λ_m) as a sensor parameter. The subscript "o" and "m" represent respectively real-life learning object and the mobile device (i.e. refers to the learner's current location). Firstly the algorithm is to compute the distance from the learner's current location to each real-life learning object. The calculation is based on the following Spherical Law of Cosines and its formula is shown in (1-0):

$$d = R * arccos [sin \phi_m * sin\varphi_o + cos \phi_m * cos\varphi_o * cos(\lambda_o - \lambda_m)] ... (1\text{-}0)$$

The ϕ_m and φ_o indicate their latitudes of the learner and the real-life learning object, the λ_m and λ_o indicate their longitudes, and the R is the radius of the earth. The distance is measured in meters. In the formula, R is a constant, R=6.371 X 10^6 meter. The geographic coordinates of the learner are acquired from the GPS receiver of the mobile device, and real-life learning object's geographic coordinates are stored in the database of the MOIAR application system. The latitude and longitude coordinates have to be converted into Radian if their unit of measure is in degree. Based on the difference of the distances from the real-life learning object to the learner, the real-life objects are filtered out if they are not within a pre-configured distance range from the learner's current location.

3.2.2 Orientation between mobile device and real-life learning object

The orientation of the mobile device defines the angle between the mobile device camera lens and the real-life learning object, which is one of calculation criteria for the content display. For example, the learner might be standing on the different side of the real-life learning object, which would require the learner to turn the camera lens to a different direction in order to get the right content to be displayed on the screen properly. As mentioned above, the mobile device's current Azimuth, each real-life leaning object's Azimuth, and the angle subtended between the two Azimuths, are the critical elements to accomplish this algorithm. The mobile device's current Azimuth is indicated as θ_m, which is also a sensor parameter and is measured in Radian, discussed in the later paragraph. Another coordinate system is the MOIAR coordinate system that based on the Cartesian coordinates, which computes the Azimuth of the each real-life learning object that is subtended to the learner's current location and the North Pole. In the MOIAR coordinate system, the learner's current location is indicated as the coordinate origin.

The MOIAR coordinate system contains two key variables. φ and λ which respectively indicate the computed West to East axis and North to South axis variables that are subtended from the learner's current location to each real-life learning object at the location. The formula for calculating the [Δφ, Δλ] is shown as follows:

$$\Delta\varphi = \varphi_0 - \phi_m \ \dots\dots\dots (1\text{-}1)$$

$$\Delta\lambda = \lambda_0 - \lambda_m \ \dots\dots\dots (1\text{-}2)$$

After [Δφ, Δλ] is computed, which indicates the new coordinate variable between the real-life learning object and the learner's current location, the Polar coordinate system is then conceptually converted into the MOIAR coordinate system, which utilizes the learner's current location as the co-ordinate origin. As mentioned above, in order to identify the right real-life object and display the right content when the learner is facing the mobile device on the right orientation to each real-life learning object, and to further guide the learner regarding which direction to face the camera lens, the Azimuth of the learner's current orientation and the Azimuth of each real-life learning object is computed. The concept of the Azimuth in the MOIAR coordinate system is shown in figure 2 and the computing formula to further calculate the Azimuth θ_c is presented as follows:

$$\tan \theta = \left|\frac{Y_c}{X_c}\right| \ \dots\dots\dots\dots\dots\dots\dots\dots\dots\dots\dots\dots\dots\dots\dots\dots\dots(1\text{-}3)$$

$$\theta = \tan^{-1}\left|\frac{Y_c}{X_c}\right| \ \dots\dots\dots\dots\dots\dots\dots\dots\dots\dots\dots\dots\dots\dots\dots(1\text{-}4)$$

$$\theta_c = 90° \text{ or } 270° \pm \theta \ \dots\dots\dots\dots\dots\dots\dots\dots\dots\dots\dots\dots\dots(1\text{-}5)$$

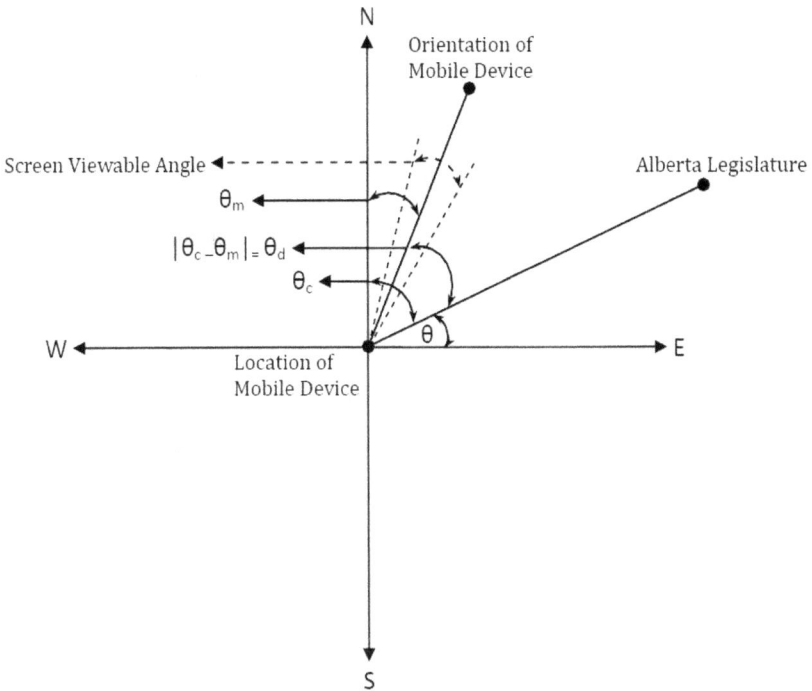

Figure 2: The concept of the MOIAR coordinate system in the algorithm

In the MOIAR coordinate system, the vertical line from the coordinate origin to the North Pole and the horizontal line from the coordinate origin to $[\Delta\varphi, \Delta\lambda]$, become an angle θ_c, which refers to the Azimuth. In order to compute θ_c, the angle θ between the learner, the real-life learning object, and the $\Delta\varphi$ axis have to be computed first by using the Tangent Trigonometric Functions. Further, according to $[\Delta\varphi, \Delta\lambda]$ that locates the quadrant in the MOIAR coordinate system, the complete Azimuth θ_c will be found. When $\Delta\varphi$ is positive and $\Delta\lambda$ is positive, it means the real-life learning object is located in the first quadrant and θ_c will be 90° + θ. When $\Delta\varphi$ is positive and $\Delta\lambda$ is negative, it means the real-life learning object is located in the fourth quadrant and θ_c will be 90° - θ. When $\Delta\varphi$ is negative and $\Delta\lambda$ is negative, it means the real-life learning object is located in the third quadrant and θc will be $270° - \theta$. When $\Delta\varphi$ is negative and $\Delta\lambda$ is positive, it means the real-life learning object is located in the second quadrant and θc will be $270° + \theta$. Table 1 displays different cases when Azimuth θc is located in each quadrant.

Table 1: Azimuths in different quadrants of the algorithm

Mobile Device Coordinate		Mobile Device Coordinate	
-	+	+	+
RLO Coordinate		RLO Coordinate	
$\theta_c = 270° + \theta$		$\theta_c = 90° - \theta$	
Mobile Device Coordinate		Mobile Device Coordinate	
-	-	+	-
RLO Coordinate		RLO Coordinate	
$\theta_c = 270° - \theta$		$\theta_c = 90° + \theta$	

The Object Identification algorithm proposed and implemented in this paper is for the MOIAR application to effectively identify the real-life learning objects based on the calculated Azimuth and the subtended angle, whatever the learners' current location and orientation are, and whenever learners change them. Unlike prior AR learning applications that require learners to stand within a certain distance from the object or focus the camera lens in front of the optical marker, the MOIAR application lets the learners walk around the real-life learning object and still see the identification tags and the adaptive learning contents, as long as the camera lens is facing the real-life learning objects. Further, the MOIAR can also guide the learner to other real-life learning objects located with the object identification tags. Also, the 5R adaptive mechanism tailored the learning contents according to the learner's learning status and the mobile device's current location status. Comparing the MOIAR approach developed in this research with prior mobile AR learning research applications, most of the prior applications can only provide learning contents based on the text-book or tailored to the object itself. The MOIAR system can not only iden-tify the objects of interest but also provides the contents of interest. The 5R adaptive mechanism helps the learners in constructing more meaning-ful knowledge because the learning process and learning contents are in-tegrated with societal culture, life-context, and personal learning prefer-ences.

Once Azimuth θ_c is computed, the last step is to compute the subtended angle. The subtended angle is computed according to the difference be-tween Azimuth of the learner's current orientation, which is sensed by the built-in digital compass on the mobile device, and the Azimuth of each real-life learning object θ_c. Further, the object identification algorithm can determine whether the object identification tags and the 5R adaptive con-tents of the object should be displayed on the screen or not, according to the formula (2) below:

$$\theta_d = |\theta_m - \theta_c| \leq R \text{ (ex: R = 5°)} \dots\dots\dots(2)$$

In the formula, θd refers to the angle difference between the Azimuth of the learner's current location and each real-life learning object. Variable R refers to the Rule in the algorithm that is used to determine the error band for displaying the object identification tags and the 5R adaptive contents. The reason to compute θd as an absolute value is that the MOIAR system should display the object identification tags and the 5R adaptive contents no matter whether the real-life learning object is on the left side or right side of the learner. For example, if θm is 45° and θc is 40°, the original θd is +5°, which means the object is slightly left to the learner. On the other hand, when θm is 45° and θc is 50°, the original θd is -5°, which means the object is slightly on the right side of the learner. If we set the rule as 5°, after computing θd with an absolute value, the object identification tags and the 5R adaptive contents would be displayed in both cases.

4   The MOIAR application implementation

This section describes how the MOIAR works in the research environment created for the purpose of demonstration through a scenario study. There are three students in this scenario. Will is currently enrolled in the English program, and he is taking course 604 "Traveling English" and he is on unit one with knowledge level one. Jimmy is currently enrolled in the Politic program, and he is taking course 704 "Politic Science" and he is on unit one with knowledge level one. Alex is currently enrolled in the Architecture program, and he is taking course 804 "Introduction to Architecture" and he is on unit one with knowledge level one. The real-life learning object is the Alberta Legislature building.

4.1 Learner authentication interface

The learner authentication interface contains two parts of information, the personal learning profile and status and the learner's current location. The screen shots are shown in figure 3. The MOIAR mobile client application shows to the learners the courses and units that they are currently learning with the MOIAR application, the knowledge level of the learning contents that they will be getting, and their mobile device's current GPS location information.

Hello! Will		Hello! Jimmy		Hello! Alex	
Program:	English	Program:	Politic	Program:	Architecture
Course:	604	Course:	704	Course:	804
Unit:	1	Unit:	1	Unit:	1
Level:	1	Level:	1	Level:	1
Latitude:	53.538984°	Latitude:	53.539305°	Latitude:	53.539333°
Longitude:	-113.507411°	Longitude:	-113.507579°	Longitude:	-113.507539°
MOIAR!	Logout	MOIAR!	Logout	MOIAR!	Logout

Figure 3: Personal learning profile and status

4.2 Location-based reality learning object identification

When the learner clicks the MOIAR button, the application will launch the object identification process powered by the Location-based Object Identification Algorithm to start identifying the real-life learning object around the learner's current location and display identification tags of the location-based learning objects as shown in figure 4.

The screenshot (4 - A) shows that the MOIAR application successfully identified one of the real-life learning objects, the Alberta Legislature Building, with the object's name and the distance displayed upon the screen. The screenshots (4 - B) and (4 - C) display different identification tags at the same location according to their orientations and motions. In screenshot (4 - B), the learner was standing in front of a house that is located at the address 2422 111B Street, where the house was 0.02 km away from the learner. When the learner faced to the house right next to it, the tag shows the neighbor house's address, the distance from the learner is now shown as 0.03 km (screenshot 4 - C). The houses are predefined and stored as a real-life learning object in the database. Further, when there are more than one object in the camera view, the MOIAR mobile application will change the size of the object identification tags according to the distance; the closer the object is to the learner, the bigger the tag will be.

4.3 The 5R adaptive learning contents

The object identification tags are touchable buttons, and the learner has just to click the tags to get the detailed learning contents. The MOIAR application can identify multiple learning objects at the same time, but the screen space on the mobile device is limited. So it is better to display only the object identification tags at first because the learners do not need to see the contents until they are right in front of a real-life learning object and are ready to learn. Figure 5 shows different location-based learning contents superimposed on the real-life learning object, the Alberta Legislature building adapted to their personal learning profiles and statuses of three learners. There are three parts of contents in the content view. The first part on the top shows the name of the learning object; the second part below shows the learner's current personal learning status, and the third part shows learning contents. As shown in figure 5, screenshot (5 - A) is tourist information of the Alberta Legislature Building for the course "Travelling English". Screenshot (5 - B) shows the political history of the building for the course "Political Science". The last screenshot (5 - C) gives the design and architectural of the building for the course "Introduction to Architecture"

75

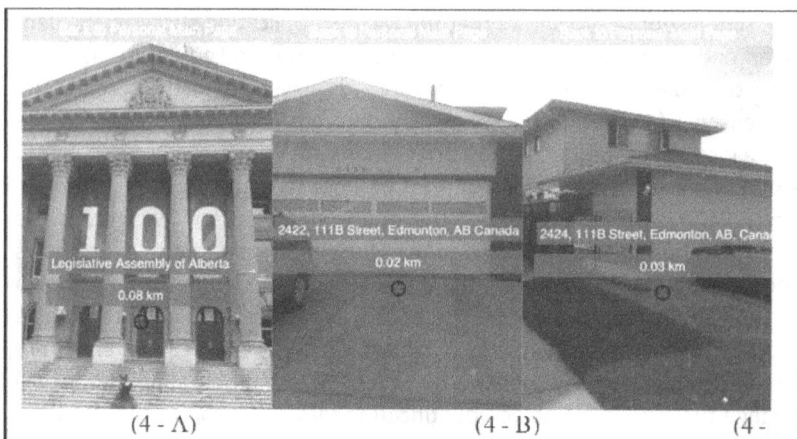

Figure 4: Location-based learning object identification tags

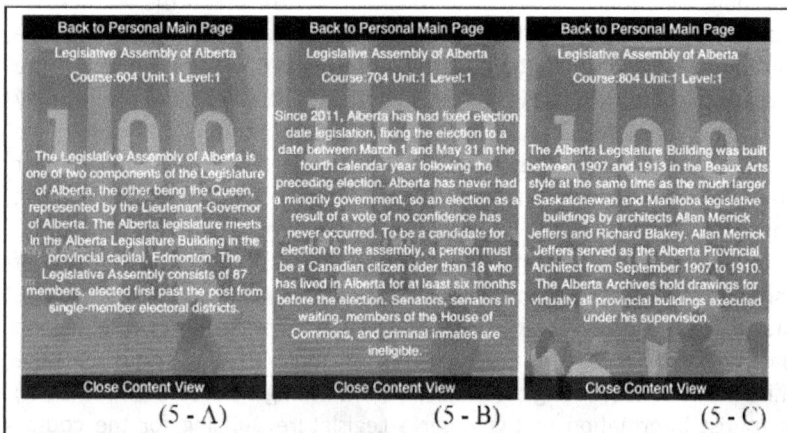

Figure 5: The 5R adaptive location-based learning contents superimposed on the real-life learning object

5   Conclusion and future work

The Location-based Object Identification algorithm presented and implemented in this paper is for the MOIAR mobile learning application to effectively identify the real-life learning objects based on the learners' current

76

location and orientation and real-life learning object's location information. The MOIAR application allows the learners walk around the real-life learning object and still see the identification tags and the adaptive learning contents, as long as the camera lens is facing the real-life learning objects. Further, the MOIAR can also guide the learner to from one real-life learning object to others marked by object identification tags. The 5R adaptive mechanism can tailor the learning contents according to the learner's learning profile and status and the mobile device's current location. The MOIAR application can not only identify the objects of interest but also provide the contents of interest. The 5R adaptive mechanism helps the learners in constructing more meaningful knowledge because the learning process and learning contents are integrated with societal culture, life-context, and personal learning preferences.

The focuses of this research are on the algorithm development and its implementation to support using AR technique in location-based mobile learning setting. Further research should be on how the AR technique enhances the mobile learning application and how the MOIAR has impacted on the learners in the mobile learning setting.,

References

Chang, W., Tan, Q. and Fang, W.T. (2010) Multi-Object Oriented Augmented Reality for Location-Based Adaptive Mobile Learning, In the proceeding of 2010 IEEE 10th International Conference on Advanced Learning Technologies, pp: 450 - 451

Chang, W. and Tan, Q. (2010) Augmented Reality System Design and Scenario Study for Location-Based Adaptive Mobile Learning, In the proceeding of 2010 IEEE 13th International Conference on Computational Science and Engineering, pp: 20 – 27

Ferscha, A. (2002) Contextware: Bridging Physical and Virtual Worlds, Reliable Software Technologies - AE2002, (invited paper), Lecture Notes in Computer Science 2361, Springer Verlag, Berlin.

Ferscha, A., Beer, W., Narzt, W. (2001) Location Awareness in Community Wireless LANs in Kurt Bauknecht, Wilfried Brauer, Thomas A. Muck (Eds.): Informatik 2001: Wirtschaft und Wissenschaft in der Network Economy - Visionen und Wirklichkeit, Tagungsband der GI/OCG-Jahrestagung, Universitat Wien, ISBN: 3-85403-157-2, Sept. 2001, pp: 190-195.

Harter, A., Hopper, A. et al.(1999) The Anatomy of A Context-Aware Application, In the Proceedings of the 5th Annual ACM/IEEE International Conference on Mobile Computing and Networking, pp 59–68.

Kalkbrenner, G. and Koppe, E. (2002) Mobile Management of Local Infrastructure, In the proceeding of the 10th International Conference on Software, telecommunications and computer networks, pp. 486-491.

Priyantha, N. B., Chakraborty, A., et al. (2000) The Cricket Location- Support System. In 6th ACM MOBICOM, Boston, MA, August, 2000.

Reitmayr, G. and Schmalstieg, D. (2003) Collaborative augmented reality for outdoor navigation and information browsing. Geowissenschaftliche Mitteilungen (Proc. 2nd Symposium on Location Based Services and TeleCartography), pp. 53-62, Vienna University of Technology, 2003. TR-188-2-2003-28, Vienna University of Technology, Dec. 2003.

Rohs, M. (2004) Real-world interaction with camera-phones, In the proceeding of 2nd International Symposium on Ubiquitous Computing Systems, Tokyo, Japan, Nov., pp 74–89.

Rohs, M.and Zweifel, P. (2005) A conceptual framework for camera phone-based interaction techniques. In Proc. Pervasive, pp 171–189, 2005.

Tan, Q., Zhang, X.K., Kinshuk, & McGreal, R. (2011) The 5R Adaptation Framework for Location-Based Mobile Learning Systems. In the proceedings of the 10th World Conference on Mobile and Contextual Learning, Beijing, China, 18-21October, 2011.

Toye, E., Sharp, R. et al. (2005) Using smart phones to access sitespecific services. IEEE Pervasive Computing, 4(2): pp. 60–66.

'I am not a Person with a Creative Mind': Facilitating Creativity in the Undergraduate Curriculum Through a Design-Based Research Approach

Denise Wood[1] and Carolyn Bilsborow[2]
[1]Central Queensland University, University of South Australia and the University of the Western Cape, South Africa
[2]University of South Australia

Originally published in ICEL (2013) Volume 12 Issue 1

Editorial commentary

Wood and Bilsborow present a challenge that most educational institutions face in terms of learning objectives: teaching creativity, or more specifically, teaching creative problem solving with active learning methods. Creativity has recently been defined as "the most important leadership quality" (IBM capitalizing on a Complexity study of 1500 CEOs in 60 countries). This is because it means thinking in a non standard way about problems and relating concepts and ideas from different perspectives; in an increasingly complex and turbulent business environment, this is an essential skill. Organizations are facing massive shifts – changes in global economic power centers, accelerated industrial transformations, growing volumes of data, the digitalization of all services and rapidly evolving customer preferences to name but a few. In this context, "what differentiates companies – and enables them to outperform others – is how they look at the problem, finding different ways to go after solving the problem and generating options and ideas that others are not aware of." (Yamashita, 2010). This article focuses on facilitating the development of creative problem solving skills by engaging students in complex learning activities. It analyses the positive impact of design-based research, an approach involving multiple iterations for designing, developing, trying out and implementing the conceptual framework.

IBM Capitalizing on Complexity Report (2010).
Retrieved from http://www-935.ibm.com/services/us/ceo/ceo study2010/index.html

Abstract: Today's graduates need the skills to enable them to 'persevere in the face of complexity and unresolvability' (McWilliam and Haukka 2008: 660), and to respond creatively in work environments that are increasingly dependent on digital technologies (Cunningham 2006). However, although many higher education institutions (HEIs) acknowledge the importance of creativity within the curriculum (McWilliam 2007a), it is argued that universities are failing to equip graduates with the creative skills they require to be effective in the workplace. Design-based learning (also referred to as learning by design) is ideally suited to facilitating the development of creative problem solving (CPS) skills by engaging students in complex learning activities involving the active construction of knowledge through a series of iterative cycles of experimentation and refinement of concepts (Naidu 2004). Similarly, design-based research (DBR) involves a series of iterative steps to design and develop learning environments and theories the design, while also informing the development of practical guidelines (Reeves, Herrington and Oliver, 2005). This paper reports on findings from a project funded by the Australian Government Office for Learning and Teaching, which aimed to develop a CPS framework and supporting online system to scaffold teachers and students through a creative problem solving approach founded on the principles of DBR. The study employed a mixed-methods DBR approach involving multiple iterations to design, develop, trial and implement the framework and tool, as well as the development of principles and practical guidelines for application in the classroom. The findings reported in this paper focus on the DBR process and the experience trialling the CPS tool in a first-year undergraduate course offered in the School of Communication, International Studies and Languages at the University of South Australia. The paper reports on the implications of the findings from the project and the benefits of DBR as a methodology informing the design, development and implementation of a technology enhanced learning approach to fostering CPS in the undergraduate curriculum.

Keywords: Creativity; Creative Problem Solving; Design-Based Research; Higher Education; Graduate Attributes; Generic Skills

80

1 Background

The need for a more creative workforce able to respond to complex and uncertain times is well established (Craft 2006; Florida 2003; McWilliam 2007a; Pink 2006). Creativity and innovation are crucial to the success of businesses in the networked information society of the 21st Century, necessitating graduates who are able to undertake creative work in environments that are increasingly dependent on digital technologies (Cunningham 2006). Recognition of the changing demands in a knowledge based economy and the need to better prepare graduates with 21st century skills (*Transforming Australia's Higher Education System* 2009) has refocused attention on the need for universities to foster the development of graduates' employability skills such as the ability to communicate effectively, solve problems, work in teams and think creatively. This emphasis is also evident in the Australian Government's HEI funding strategy, with its focus on the employability of graduates and the production of graduates who are 'work ready' (Harvey & Shahjahan 2013).

The Australian Government has also highlighted the central role that creativity plays as the driver of social and economic success. In a report arising from the Australia 2020 Summit held in 2008, 'creativity, interpretation, innovation and cultural understanding' are identified as core skills required by the industries of the 21st century' (*Responding to the Australia 2020 Summit* 2009: 193). Yet despite this recognition of the central role of creativity and innovation in the workplace, many argue that universities are failing to equip their graduates with these skills (Craft 2006; Tosey 2006). Moreover, although creativity, creative thinking and innovation are generic skills required for life-long learning, as with many other generic skills identified by employers, these skills do not feature in any Australian graduate attributes statements (Oliver 2011). Although HEIs acknowledge the importance of creativity within the curriculum (McWilliam 2007b), many programs focus on particular kinds of graduate attributes and traditional educational approaches, rather than employability skills relating to creative thinking and creative problem solving (Gluth and Corso 2009; Wood et. al. 2011; Wood et. al. 2015). There are also many pressures on teachers in HEIs, where there in an intolerance to ambiguity, lack of time and space for experimentation, fear of making mistakes, high levels of stress, and the lack of a sense of challenge (Byron 2007), which contribute further to their resistance to embedding creativity in the curriculum. Emphasis in education has been mostly concerned with what De Bono (1973) calls vertical thinking; the process of proving and developing concept patterns, whereas lateral or creative thinking sets out to restructure such patterns and provoke new ones.

One of the major barriers facing teachers wishing to incorporate creative approaches in their teaching and learning has been the lack of explicit guidelines and a scaffold to guide them in making the required shift from outmoded teaching approaches to more innovative approaches to embedding creativity within the curriculum. This is especially so in discipline areas outside of design and the arts (Gluth and Corso, 2009). Tosey (2006: 35) suggests that creativity in the higher education curriculum is more often used 'to converge and control' than to engage productively 'at the edge of order' (Fullan, cited in Tosey 2006: 34). To change this prevailing culture, argues Jackson (2006), we need to change our approach from penalising mistakes to one of appreciating that making 'mistakes' provides important lessons for learning. 'By perceiving 'mistakes' as opportunities for, and proof of, learning instead of failure, we begin to change the paradigm to one that is more enabling and valuing of creative effort' (Jackson 2006: 197).

Another potential reason that universities have failed to embrace creativity in the curriculum more widely across different disciplinary fields is the lack of a concise definition of creativity within policy documentation (McWilliam 2007a). Edwards (2000) suggests that the term 'creativity' has an amorphous nature; a gift that is only possessed by an exceptional few. However, research has drawn attention to the importance of fostering the creativity of all learners (Csikszentmihalyi 1982; McWilliam 2007a). Researchers are also challenging the assumption that creativity is purely an innate capacity and cannot be learned (McWilliam 2007a; Robinson 2001), and they have demonstrated that human intelligence is complex and multifaceted (Robinson, 2001). Creativity is enhanced by other capacities and learner motivations and also influenced by the cultural context; cultural conditions can kindle or kill creativity (Robinson, 2001).

A third barrier to changing the educational paradigm in ways that foster the creative capacities of future graduates relates to the lack of strategies to help teachers develop the skills to engage with creativity 'intentionally

as an outcome of pedagogical work' (McWilliam 2007a: 4). Fostering creativity is 'best achieved through a process-based or activity-based curriculum that engages students in challenging, novel and unpredictable ways of
working and learning' (Jackson 2003 cited in Jackson 2006: 213), however,
the strategies for achieving this goal are less evident for teachers. The following sections outline an approach aimed at addressing these three barriers through the design and development of a CPS framework and associated tools to provide a scaffold to teachers in the design of their curricula,
and to guide students in applying the skills of creative problem solving in
their studies.

2   A systems approach to creativity

Creativity is the process of creating novel and useful ideas or products
(Dewett 2003). Although creativity can be learned and assessed, the learning environment will either facilitate or impede the achievement of creative performance. A CPS framework needs to be able to be adapted to suit
the domain and field of study, while also accommodating individual student needs by taking into consideration their abilities and preferred learning styles. Such a framework also needs to optimise the opportunities both
divergent and convergent thinking, risk taking, evaluating decisions, and
synthesising existing and new information in order to arrive at an optimal
outcome. Finally, the framework should address strategies to maximise the
conditions under which the experience of learning will be its own reward
(referred to by Csikszentmihalyi (1996) as being in the 'flow').

Amabile (1996) identifies three components of creative performance: 1)
domain-relevant skills; 2) creativity-relevant processes; and 3) task motivation. Such an approach is consistent with Csikszentmihalyi's (1999) systems
approach in recognising that domain-relevant skills (for example, facts,
principles, technical skills, and opinions) are required for a student to be
able to assess the range of response possibilities and to be able to synthe-
sise the information against which the new response is to be judged (Csikszentmihalyi 1999; Dewett 2003). Creativity-relevant processes determine
the degree to which a student's response will surpass previous responses
in the domain (Dewett 2003), while task motivation refers to the student's
attitude and motivations for undertaking the task, as well as his/her understanding about why the task is being engaged (Amabile 1996; Dewett
2003). Again, consistent with (Csikszentmihalyi (1991), Amabile agrees that

creativity is more likely to be facilitated when the task is intrinsically moti-vating (the experience of learning is its own reward) (Csikszentmihalyi 1991).

The principles of CPS have been attributed to the pioneering work of Alex Osborn who developed the approach as an aid to the understanding the different phases of creative problem-solving (Isaksen and Dorval 1993). The Osborn-Parnes CPS model is a modification of Osborn's CPS approach, comprising three major stages:1) exploring the challenge; 2) generating ideas; and 3)preparing for action, and six steps within those stages: 1) ob-jective finding; 2) fact finding; 3) problem finding; 4) generating ideas; 5) solution finding; and 6) acceptance finding (Creative Education Foundation 2010). This model is depicted as a cycle, recognising the need for flexibility and that creativity tends to function in a more cyclical than linear pattern. Variations of the model have been used across a range of disciplinary fields and for various purposes including the development of educational mate-rials (Torrance 1978), to facilitate inclusive education (Giangreco et al. 1994), and as a framework to support the marketing curriculum (Titus 2000). Amabile's (1996) componential framework of creativity incorpo-rates a similar CPS approach, but in this approach, the components of the creative performance (domain-relevant skills, creativity-relevant processes and task motivation) that impact on the individual's creative performance are also considered. All CPS approaches acknowledge the iterative nature of the problem solving process and the need for both divergent thinking (particularly during the early stages of the cycle) and convergent thinking as ideas are further refined.

3   Design-based research (DBR) approach

Design-based research emerged as a methodological approach in the 1990s (Brown 1992; Collins 1992) in response to the need for educational research that produces 'new theories, artifacts, and practices that account for and potentially impact learning and teaching in naturalistic settings' (Barab and Squire 2004: 3). DBR addresses complex problems in real con-texts, builds on theory and design principles to implement technology en-hanced innovations to address the identified complex problems and in-volves reflective inquiry in the process of designing, trialling and imple-menting innovative learning environments. DBR differs from action re-search in that DBR should result in the creation of new design principles and practical guidelines for teachers (Anderson and Shattuck 2012; Barab and Squire, 2004; Reeves, Herrington and Oliver 2005). The Design-Based Research Collective (2003) identifies five characteristics of DBR:

- The process of designing learning environments and developing theories are central to the approach
- The research process involves continuous iterative cycles of design, enactment, analysis, and redesign
- The research leads to theories that are of relevance to teachers and educational designers
- The research is undertaken in 'authentic; settings and documents the successes, failures and interactions in the local context to better understand the implications for applying in other contexts
- The methods connect processes of enactment to outcomes

DBR was chosen as the research approach for the study reported in this paper, and in keeping with the characteristics of DBR, our research team comprised teachers, researchers and designers working in collaboration and the research approach employed mix-methods with multiple iterations involving designing, developing, trialling, evaluating, reflecting and redesigning informed by the previous iteration.

3.1   Research method

The project commenced in October 2011 and completed in 2014. The initial project aims were to design and develop a CPS framework (http://www.creativity-project.net/cpsframework.php) and open source online CPS tools to act as a scaffold for teachers in the development and redevelopment of courses (Ingenium Teacher's Tool) and a CPS tool for students (Ingenium Student's Tool) to guide them through the creative problem solving process in their coursework. The project also aimed to develop guidelines, case studies of the use of CPS in courses across a range of disciplinary fields and a suite of resources available via the project site.

The research approach involved six major stages reported in the following sections. While the CPS tools were trialled in ten courses, this paper reports the findings from only one of the courses; an undergraduate course, *Introduction to Digital Media*, undertaken by students enrolled in various undergraduate programs in the School of Communication, International

Studies and Languages at the University of South Australia. The findings of the trials of the CPS tools in all ten courses are documented in full in the final report (Wood et al, in press). Details of each of the stages undertaken are presented in the following sections.

3.1.1   The design of a CPS model

The first stage of the research involved the design of the CPS model and framework informed by theories of creativity. The team drew on the seminal literature on creativity (Csikszentmihalyi 1982, 1991, 1996; Torrance 1978) and contemporary research such as Amabile's (1996) componential framework of creativity and Titus's (2000) CPS model in the design of the CPS framework and model. The adapted model developed for the study involves six stages (Figure 1), which correspond closely to the Titus (2000) model.

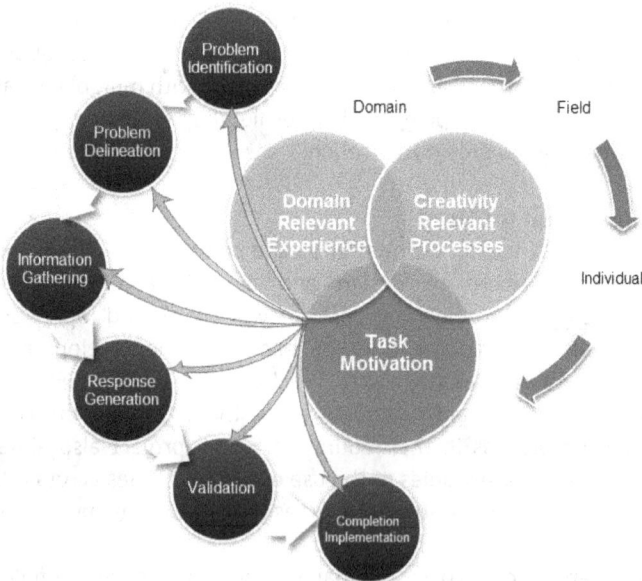

Figure 1: A Systems Approach to Creative Problem Solving (CPS) adapted from Amabile (1996), Csikszentmihalyi (1999) and Titus (2000)

However, in our adapted model we use the term 'response generation' rather than 'idea generation' for the fourth stage of the process because we view idea generation as fundamental to each stage of the creative problem solving process. Thus, idea generation is embedded in each stage of the process with alternating divergent and convergent ideation, shifting toward convergent thinking by the final stages of validation and completion/implementation (Brophy 1998). Our model also recognises the impact o f the domain, field, and individual factors (Csikszentmihalyi 1999).

3.1.2 The development of a CPS framework

The model developed during the first stage of the research process provided a conceptual overview of the processes involved in creative problem solving as well as the factors likely to impact on the way in which students engage with the approach. This model informed the development of a CPS framework incorporating the major stages of the creative process with associated practical techniques to guide teachers, and support students undertaking activities requiring them to apply the principles in practice. The techniques have been adapted from the idea generation techniques informed by the work of (Titus 2000), Gluth and Corso (2009) and The Global Creativity Corporation. The framework shown in Table 1 condenses the six stages identified in the CPS model into five major steps: 1) problem identification; 2) problem delineation; 3) information gathering; 4) experimentation and validation and implementation. Each stage in the CPS framework incorporates a list of techniques designed to assist students in generating ideas, classified according to whether the techniques involve visioning, modifying, exploring, or experimenting.

Table 1: Framework for Creative Problem-Solving using Idea Generation Techniques

CPS Stages	Idea Generation (ideation) Techniques			
	Visioning	Modifying	Exploring/Discovering	Experimenting
Problem Identification	Fluency of ideas involving generation of large number of possibilities Brainstorming Use of guided imagery Collaborating and discussing to generate ideas Using social media to enable community to submit their ideas Using blog to reflect	Refining what others have done using SCAMPER technique: (s)ubstituting (co)mbining (a)dapting (m)odifying (p)ut to use (e)liminating (r)arranging Modifying ideas based on peer feedback and discussion Using social media to create mash-ups of ideas	Cross referencing items either randomly or systematically demands new possibilities Sensory Activity to facilitating exploring the problem and subsequent possible solutions Using analogies and metaphors making associations that create more than the sum of two ideas	Removing inhibitors increasing participants' confidence to explore and try things when the outcomes are not always clear and they're conditioned to having to come up with the single 'right' answer

CPS Stages	Idea Generation (ideation) Techniques			
	Visioning	Modifying	Exploring/Discovering	Experimenting
Problem Delineation	Intuition to understand the bigger picture Refining the problem Deconstructing the problem Mind mapping Storyboarding Using blog to refine thinking and reflect	SCAMPER – combining the deconstructed components in new ways Challenging assumptions to break patterns of behaviour and facilitating the unexpected Random Association to make connections between things even when they are not apparent	Using intuition as springboard for exploration Refining ideas through discovery Using intuition to question assumptions and refine thinking about the problem	Assessing components to identify "leverage points" and opportunities for new approaches

CPS Stages	Idea Generation (ideation) Techniques			
	Visioning	Modifying	Exploring/Discovering	Experimenting
Information Gathering	Seeking information on the big picture and component parts guided by intuition and refinement of the problem Using blog to capture thoughts and document research findings Sharing findings via wiki and bookmarking sites	Considering multiple sources and then looking for springboards to new sources – forming new associations Modifying research strategy as ideas are refined Analysing information to identify priorities, possibilities and areas for further research	Challenging assumptions to generate new ways of addressing the research process Undertaking research using a variety of sources (Web, social media, library, databases, broadcast media, primary sources) and then refining research process Seeking different sources of information	Combining findings from sources to help refine the solution or to generate new ideas to springboard further areas and sources for research

CPS Stages	Idea Generation (ideation) Techniques			
	Visioning	Modifying	Exploring/Discovering	Experimenting
Experimentation and Validation	Using visionary techniques to generate and identify problem to come up with novel solutions Using blog to document experiments and reflect on the outcomes Collaborating via blog and discussion forum	Moving from divergent manipulations of information to convergent refinement to focus on practical solutions	Risk taking and making mistakes to explore possibilities without penalty if they don't work, leading to refinement and weighing up the solutions to arrive at practical solutions	Risk taking and making mistakes without penalty if they fail, leading to refinement and weighing up the solutions to arrive at practical solutions Building on solutions more likely to lead to success
Implementation	'Produsage' using social media Discussion, peer review, web metrics, formal evaluation Personal blog for reflection on process Public blog for gaining feedback	Modifying approach if initial implementation needs further refinement	Exploring the unique contribution the innovation has made through market research and evaluation	Evaluating and examining success and identifying areas for future improvement.

3.1.3 Trials of the CPS framework in a first-year undergraduate course

Introduction to Digital Media (IDM) is a first year undergraduate course offered in the School of Communication, International Studies and Languages at the University of South Australia. The aim of the course is to introduce students to the principles of digital media through a practice-led research approach. Prior attempts at engaging students in research had proved challenging (see Wood 2010; Wood & Bilsborow, 2013 for detailed discussion of the results of formal evaluations).

The three assignments in the course build on each other and are designed to lead students through a practice-based research approach involving researching the needs of a not-for-profit organisation and producing pre-production documentation for a short promotional video clip for that organisation as the second assignment. Students then produce an associated website in which the promotional clip is embedded as their final assignment.

In the 2009 and 2010 offerings of the course students were asked to formulate their research using a paper-based version of the CPS framework designed to guide them through the idea generation process. A range of social media tools were utilised in the course: an 'ideas journal' students maintained as a personal blog throughout the course; a wiki to facilitate brainstorming and to encourage collaborative discussion; a discussion forum for peer review; a collaborative bookmarking site for sharing resources; and a YouTube channel, for showcasing student work to a broader audience.

Several emergent themes from the application of CPS in this course (see also Wood 2010; Wood and Bilsborow 2013) were noted based on teachers' informal feedback and student course evaluations conducted at the completion of each offering of the course:

- Teachers reported much greater creativity and divergence in the approaches students adopted in their digital media research assignments
- Students reported greater confidence in their ability to generate ideas for their research projects

- Several students noted that CPS was critical to the success of their research
- Most students enjoyed the collaboration with their peers and noted that the use of peer review facilitated via the discussion forum helped them to improve on their work
- One student suggested that 'I thoroughly enjoyed this topic as it was highly creative and we were given a high degree of creative freedom despite having to work within the limitations set down'
- Another commented 'The creativity component challenged my technical ability' and another reflected on the link between research and creative thinking, 'It was more research based and required a lot of creative thinking'
- Creativity and problem solving developed through practice-led research was a commonly recurring theme in most student comments as this student's feedback indicates, 'Creative idea generation methods ... helped me to think very deeply and come up with alternative and sophisticated solutions to creative problems'

Most students welcomed the brainstorming approach to idea generation implemented early in the course, however, two students commented that it was just 'mind mapping' and nothing particularly innovative; even though they acknowledged that the approach might be useful for 'other' students, 'It might work for some people but not so well for others. Only really suits a few types of learners'. Another challenge encountered in using the 'ideas' blog for scaffolding throughout the IDM course, was the tendency for some students to post their reflections to their blogs in the week 'in the flow' to maintain focus on the creative problem solving process throughout the duration of the semester.

3.1.4 Design of the CPS tool

The CPS framework therefore required considerable revisions over time, and as noted in the more detailed case studies reported elsewhere (see Wood 2010; Wood & Bilsborow 2013; Wood et al in press), the outcomes from each subsequent offering helped to improve on the approach throughout 2011.

An online tool (*Ingenium*) was designed in late 2011 based on the paper-based version of the CPS framework. This version of *Ingenium* incorporated the five stages of the CPS process with sub-sections comprising questions and prompts related to each of the five stages, which students access via arrows on each page (see Figure 2). Video clips were also included for each CPS stage to help guide students through the required tasks relevant to that stage. A pencil icon provided students with a link to a public blog site where they could set up and access their own blog account and another icon ('w') provides students with a link through to the project wiki. A menu was placed on the right-hand side of the interface providing students with a series of creativity tools including a 'notebook', 'toolbox' and 'resources' as well (see Figure 2). These sections included the social media and other supporting resources that the user might need throughout the creative solving process.

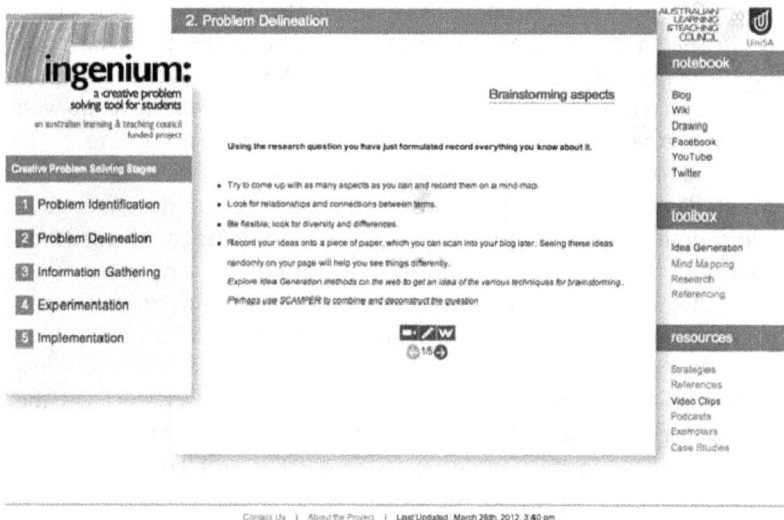

Figure 2: Design of first iteration of the CPS *Ingenium* tool

3.1.5 The redesign of Ingenium over successive iterations following a DBR approach

The DBR approach implemented in this study involved a research team comprising teachers, researchers and designers working in collaboration and the research approach employed mix-methods with multiple iterations involving designing, developing, trialling, evaluating, reflecting and redesigning informed by the previous iteration. The approach aimed to be consistent with the characteristics of DBR identified by The Design-Based Research Collective (2003) and follow the guidelines proposed by Reeves, Herrington and Oliver (2005). Details of the iterative cycles of design and redesign informed by the findings of a series of trial of the CPS tool over several offerings of the course are reported in detail in the following sections and also documented elsewhere (see for example Wood & Bilsborow, 2013; Wood et al, in press).

Preliminary trials of *Ingenium* were conducted in both semester one (Study Period 2; SP2) and semester two (Study Period 5; SP5) 2012. At the conclusion of the SP2 offering of the course, students were invited to complete the university's approved anonymous online course evaluation. The evaluation included three custom open-ended text questions: 1) *Did the creative problem solving process assist you in generating ideas for your topic and production?* 2) *Did you find the blog a useful approach to maintaining your journal of creative thinking and research?* 3) *What were your experiences using the creativity tool to generate your ideas?*

Of the 250 students enrolled in the course, only 19 (7.6%) completed the online evaluation and even fewer responded to the open-ended questions. Nevertheless, student feedback combined with teachers' observations and reflections on the experience did provide insight into the potential benefits and challenges in applying the tool in this first year course. Positive comments suggested that the course encouraged students to explore creativity in ways that they had not experienced in courses with more traditional assignments. Comments such as the statement by one student that 'It was a good course to express creativity through a different format, one that was more interesting than just the regular essay writing in others', and another who stated that 'it helped to clarify the idea I had' suggest that the approach had the desired impact. However, several students approached the task with a more closed mind and did not engage in the creative problem solving task as indicated by comments such as 'No, everyone already had their ideas to start with and in doing this did not further develop them or create them'. Some students also expressed frustration with the repetitive nature of the process indicating that the tool had not adequately reinforced the value of creativity occurring through a process of multiple iterations involving research, design, testing, refinement, collaboration and reflection.

Ingenium was trialled again in the same course in SP5 2012. At the conclusion of this offering of the course, students were again invited to complete the same anonymous online survey. Twenty-seven students responded and of those, 48% reported that *Ingenium* raised their awareness of creative problem solving and helped them to think more creatively about their assignment; 41% indicated that they felt *Ingenium* would be useful to other areas of their studies; and 33% of students reported that they felt more confident about their creative skills after using *Ingenium*.

While one student 'Found the tool a great catalyst for new directions in thinking ...' and another reported that it was a 'Very good planning tool', others were challenged by the presentation of the interface as suggested by one student who commented 'I found the site rather hard to use. It was hard to follow the layout of the information and contained a lot of writing that could be cut down to be more accessible and concise'. Students were also challenged by the amount of time it took to complete the process, as comments such as 'The principles and techniques are good, but the presentation and long winded nature make it unusable' and 'Thought it was very useable it was also slightly daunting because of the amount of subsections ... this is incredibly tedious to work through' suggest. When asked what improvements should be made to the tool students suggested: 'Better structural layout'; 'Include some visuals ...'; '... perhaps find another way of presenting'; 'It needs a complete overhaul design wise'.

Based on the feedback from two semesters of trials in IDM in 2012, *Ingenium* was redesigned to include new video examples and text-based instructions (see Figure 3). During the SP5 2012 trial, one teacher observed that students were not using the example videos noting 'The students would begin playing the video and only watch it for a few seconds before closing it'. To address this issue, the 'talking-head' videos were replaced with short animations, designed to explain the stages of *Ingenium* in a more engaging manner.

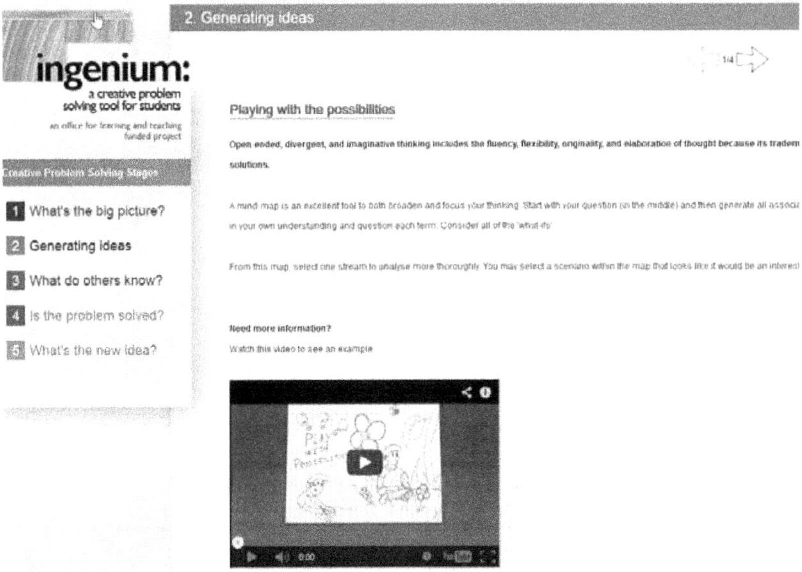

Figure 3: Redesigned CPS tool with embedded video examples

The text component of the tool was also redesigned during this version in response to student feedback suggesting that the language used was too abstract and not descriptive of the process. For example, 'Problem Delineation' was changed to 'What's the big picture?' The procedural text descriptions were also simplified to address student feedback suggesting that the steps were too repetitive and long-winded.

The structure of *Ingenium* was also redesigned as a mind map (Figure 4) to provide a more creative, non-linear approach to the structure.

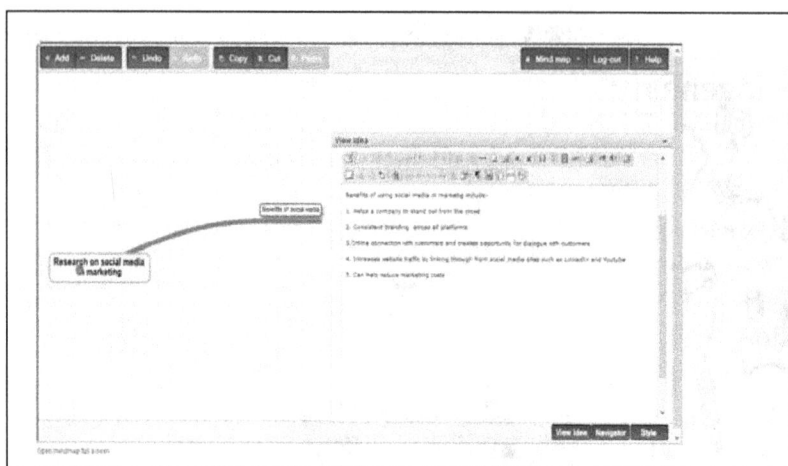

Figure 4: Redesigned CPS tool with mind map interface

A new group of students enrolled in IDM undertook the same assignment to create the pre-production for a promotional video clip in the first semester (SP2) 2013. The students were encouraged to use the new mind mapping tool that would allow them to access the process in a non-linear fashion, but during the trial, technical issues with the mind mapping tool were encountered and many of the students were forced to return to the original linear, step by step instruction approach.

Sixty-two students responded to the online survey and their responses indicated an increase in the percentage of students who indicated that their awareness of creative problem solving had been improved through using the tool (48% in SP5 2012 to 55% in SP2 2013). Fifty-one percent of students reported that the tool had helped them think creatively compared with 48% during the previous trial, and 33% of students reported that they felt more confident about their creative skills after using the *Ingenium*, which remained the same as during the previous trial

Many students responded favourably to the redesigned video examples with comments such as 'The YouTube videos linked to the pages were useful' and one teacher observed that unlike the previous trials, more students watched the videos in their entirety. However, several issues were encountered by the students as reflected by comments such as: 'The mind map ... is a useful tool, but very unreliable'; 'I liked how *Ingenium* was easy to use, however, I was not pleased with my mind map being entirely deleted days before my assignment was due'; and 'it would have been wicked, but it crashed a lot'. When asked what improvements should be made to the tool students reported that 'the menu structure should be made more easy to understand'; "it just needs to be fine-tuned so that the questions are less repetitive and the mind-mapping section works'; and 'work primarily on the user interface and the rest will come, as will interest'.

The student feedback from the three trials of *Ingenium* reported in the previous sections informed the next iteration of the design and development cycle. The major revisions included a move to a more robust approach to coding the site to avoid cross-browser issues, the redesign of the entire interface as a mind map with engaging graphics representing each stage of the CPS and each sub-section (Figure 5).

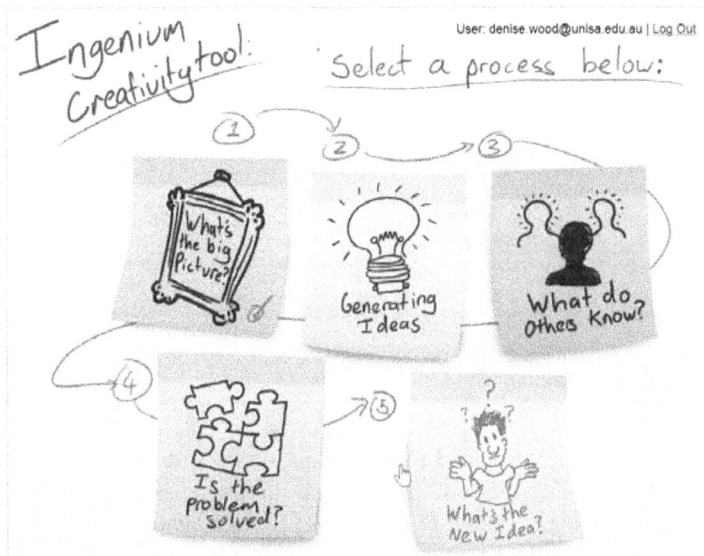

Figure 5: Revised Ingenium mind mapping tool

Students interact with each of the 'post-it' note image links to progress to sub-sections of each CPS stage and can embed their thoughts, research, images and links within the clouds relating to each sub-section. A toolbar above *Ingenium* provides students with the ability to navigate back and forth in a linear or non-linear approach as they work through the CPS stages. Students can also print out a report of their progress in outline format (Figure 6).

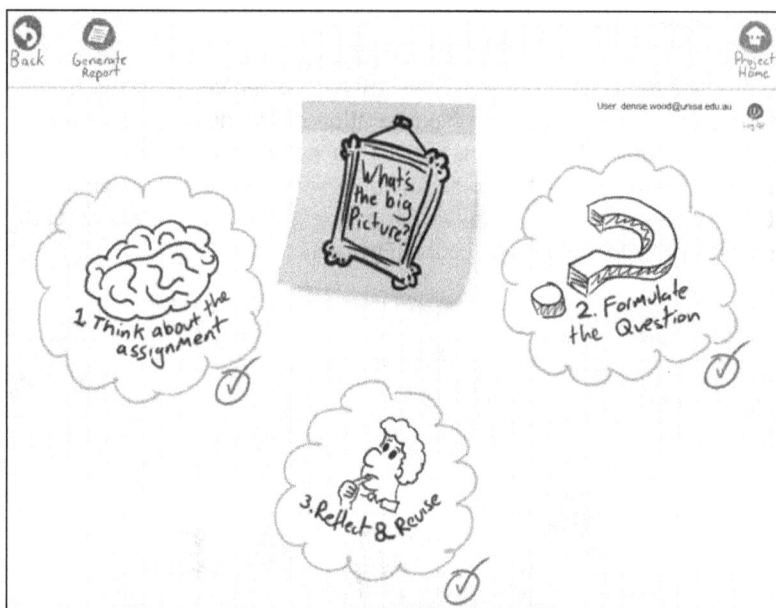

Figure 6: Revised *Ingenium* with report generator button

The revised *Ingenium* tool was trialled during the SP5, 2013 offering of IDM. Eight students responded to the online survey after completing their first assignment using the tool. Once again, there was diversity in experiences reported. Some students enjoyed the process as reflected by comments such as, 'it enabled me to think outside the box in relation to my topic and brought forward some really valuable ideas' and 'I liked *Ingenium* as I am not a person with a creative mind'. But several students noted there were too many repetitive steps involved as indicated by comments suggesting 'I liked the way that it stepped through each stage, but I believe the number of steps needed to complete was time consuming'. Similarly, one student stated that 'there are too many sections which means you are constantly repeating yourself, also it is not clear what to put in each section' and another suggested that 'a danger was to spend far too much time filling in the various boxes/bubbles. It could very easily eat up time'.

Beyond the mechanics of the tool students reflected on how *Ingenium* allowed them to combine the processes of research and creativity. One student reported, 'I found it interesting that we were asked to brainstorm, write down assumptions and deconstruct/reconstruct first then to do further research. Usually it is the other way around. I liked this approach as I didn't have any pre conceived ideas or restrictions influencing my ideas, I do wonder how my ideas would have differed if I had researched first'. Often considered as two distinct stages, research and creative problem solving are brought together in this tool, enabling students to see the complementarity of the processes.

The feedback from many iterations of the DBR process indicates that there are still some issues to be resolved, particularly with respect to the repetitive nature of the steps. Based on the findings of these trials, further revisions are in progress reduce the requirement for students to complete reflective notes at the completion of each sub-section within the major stages of the CPS process. Rather, they will complete the sub-sections and then summarise their reflections for that stage of the process before moving on to the next stage. This revision will allow users to skip over the sub-steps that they feel are unnecessary. The revised version of *Ingenium* will be trialled in IDM during the first semester of 2014 and reported in future publications.

3.1.6   *Design of guidelines informed by the findings*
As noted in the preceding sections, an important feature of DBR is that the research results in the development of guidelines for use by other teachers. The guidelines arising from this study are documented in detail in the final report (Wood et al, in press), and include guidelines for planning to teach creative problem solving, strategies for teaching creative problem solving, and appropriate alternative approaches to assessing creativity. A brief summary of the guidelines follows:

Planning to teach creative problem solving: This set of guidelines acknowledges that changing to a new teaching method takes flexibility and practice, and a commitment to transforming the teaching and learning approach from teacher-centred to student-centred. The approach highlights the benefits of engaging students in activities in which they learn by design recognising that graduates need skills that enable them to respond to complexity and uncertainty in the workplace, and that skills require a level of tacit knowing and confidence that cannot be acquired from reading through the process alone.

Teaching creative problem solving: These guidelines emphasise the importance of teaching the value of creativity, valuing exploration and mistakes, building on students' interests, enhancing opportunities for student collaboration, and embedding reflective practice in the curriculum.

Assessing creativity: Many teachers are unsure of how to assess creativity; however, alternative assessment approaches such as self- and peer-assessment are well suited as they encourage reflection and collaboration. Another important feature of assessing creativity is to focus on the process, rather than the end product; rewarding students for experimentation and learning from their mistakes through critical reflection on the process and acting on what they learn through the journey is in many ways more important than the final product arising from that process.

4 Conclusion

The study reported in this paper aimed to address the three major challenges affecting the capacity of teachers to incorporate creative problem solving approaches into their teaching and learning. These three challenges include the lack of an appropriate model to support them in making the required shift from outmoded pedagogical methodologies to more creative approaches; the lack of a concise definition of creativity within policy documentation; and the lack of strategies to help teachers develop the skills to engage with creativity in their teaching and learning. The study involved developing a CPS framework and associated tools designed to scaffold students through the creative problem solving process and guide teachers in the design and redevelopment of the curriculum.

Denise Wood and Carolyn Bilsborow

The DBR approach applied in the project ensured that the development of the CPS tools was responsive to student and teacher feedback through multiple iterations involving design, development, trials, evaluation, collaboration, reflection and revision. Consistent with a DBR approach, the research built on a strong theoretical foundation informed by creativity theories and contemporary research showing the benefits of creative problem solving in education (Amabile 1996; Robinson 2001; Titus 2006; Tosey 2000) and practical techniques to guide teachers, and support students undertaking creative problem solving activities (Titus 2000; The Global Creativity Corporation). The DBR approach is not without its challenges (see for example Anderson and Shattuck 2012; Barab and Squire 2004), as the highly critical feedback by students to early iterations suggest. However, the approach is appropriate for research that seeks to address 'real-world' problems through an iterative research process, which systematically refines the design, while also leading to the production of design principles and practical guidelines (Amiel and Reeves 2008: 34).

The study also highlights the value in students being integrally involved in the design and development of technology enhanced learning innovations. As the feedback documented in the preceding sections demonstrate, without such rich formative feedback, it would not have been possible to develop a CPS tool that meets the needs of students from diverse backgrounds. Moreover, as we came to realise when students started using the tool in their assignments, the DBR approach reflects the approach students themselves are undertaking in their assignments through the design based learning approach employed in the course. Therefore, an unintended benefit from the adoption of DBR as our preferred research design has been the enhancement of our understanding of the similarities between DBR as a research approach and design based learning, which in turn, is reflected in the final design of the CPS tool. As Vogt et al (2010) suggest, 'learning by designing' can facilitate deep learning and competence development through a complex series of activities involving students in the process of information gathering, problem identification and constraint setting, idea generation, modelling and prototyping, building, and evaluating.

The focus of this paper has been on the application of DBR to the design and development of a CPS framework and tool to support students. Al-

103

though only one case study (a first-year undergraduate course) is reported in this paper, the same process has been applied in the trials of all 10 courses that were included in the study. Furthermore, this paper only reports the findings from trials of the CPS tool with students, even though the aim of the project was to design and develop a framework and tools to both scaffold teachers in the design of their courses and guide students in the application of creative problem solving within their courses. Research involving trials of the CPS tool with teachers are currently underway to assess the extent to which the framework and tool is effective in facilitating the kind of transformation in teaching practice required to support teachers in engaging with creativity 'intentionally as an outcome of pedagogical work' (McWilliam 2007a, p. 4).

5 Acknowledgements

Support for the research reported in his paper has been provided by the Australian Government Office for Learning and Teaching. The views expressed in this publication/activity do not necessarily reflect the views of the Australian Government Office for Learning and Teaching.

References

Amabile, T. M. (1996) Creativity in context: Update to the social psychology of creativity, Boulder, CO: Westview.

Amiel, T. and Reeves, T. (2008) 'Design-based research and educational technology: Rethinking technology and the research agenda', Journal of Educational Technology & Society, vol. 11, no. 4, pp. 29-40.

Anderson, T & Shattuck, J 2012, 'Design-Based Research: A Decade of Progress in Education Research?', Educational Researcher, vol. 41, no. 1, 2012, pp. 16-25.

Barab, S. and Squire, K. (2004) 'Design-based research: Putting a stake in the ground', Journal of the Learning Sciences, vol. 13, no. 1, pp. 1-14.

Brophy, D. R. (1998) 'Understanding, measuring, and enhancing individual creative problem-solving efforts', Creativity Research Journal, vol.11, no. 2, p. 123.

Brown, A. (1992) 'Design experiments: Theoretical and methodological challenges in creating complex interventions in classroom settings', The Journal of the Learning Sciences, vol. 2, no. 2, pp. 141-178.

Byron, K. (2007). Defining boundaries for creativity. Proceedings of creativity or conformity? Building cultures for creativity in higher education conference, University of Cardiff.

Collins, A. (1992) 'Towards a design science of education', in Scanlon, E. & O'Shea, T. (eds.) New Directions in Educational Technology, Springer, Berlin, pp. 15-22.

Craft, A. (2006) 'Creativity in schools', in Jackson, N. et al (eds.), Developing Creativity in Higher Education: An Imaginative Curriculum, Routledge, London, pp. 19-28.

Creative Education Foundation (2010) What is CPS? [Online], Available: http://www.creativeeducationfoundation.org/?page_id=41 [27 Dec 2010].

Czikszentmihalyi, M. (1982) 'Intrinsic motivation and effective teaching: A flow analysis', New Directions for Teaching and Learning, vol. 10, pp. 15-26.

Csikszentmihalyi, M. (1991) 'Thoughts about education', Creating the Future: Perspectives on Educational Change, pp. 83–86.

Csikszentmihalyi, M. (1996) Creativity: flow and the psychology of discovery and invention, New York: Harper Collins.

Csikszentmihalyi, M. (1999) 'Implications of a systems perspective for the study of creativity', in Sternberg, R. (ed.), Handbook of Creativity, UK: Cambridge University Press.

Cunningham, S. (2006) What price a creative economy? Sydney: Currency House.

De Bono, E. (1973) Lateral thinking: Creativity step by step. New York: Harper Paperbacks.

Dewett, T. (2003) Understanding the relationship between information technology and creativity in organizations, Creativity Research Journal, vol. 15, no. 2/3, p. 167.

Edwards, S. M. (2000) 'The technology paradox: Efficiency versus creativity', Creativity Research Journal, vol. 13, no. 2, pp. 221-228.

Florida, R. (2003) The rise of the creative class: and how it's transforming work, leisure, community and everyday life, Victoria: Pluto Press.

Giangreco, M. Cloninger, C. Dennis, R., & Edelman, S. (1994) 'Problem-solving methods to facilitate inclusive education', in Villa, V. R. and Nevin, A. I. (eds.), Creativity and Collaborative Learning: A Practical Guide to Empowering Students and Teachers, Baltimore: Paul H. Brookes Publishing, pp. 321-346.

Gluth, S. and Corso, R. (2009) 'The application of creative thinking methodologies to post graduate entrepreneurship education', Sixth Annual AGSE International Entrepreneurship and Innovation Research Exchange Proceedings, Adelaide.

Harvey, N. and Shahjahan, M. (2013) Employability of Bachelor of Arts graduates, Sydney: Office for Learning and Teaching.

Isaksen, S. and Dorval, K. (1993) Changing views of creative problem solving: Over 40 years of continuous improvement [Online], Available: http://www.buffalostate.edu/orgs/cbir/readingroom/html/Isaksen-Dorval-93.html [28 Dec 2010].

Jackson, N. (2006) 'Imagining a different world', in Jackson, N., Oliver, M., Shaw, M. and Wisdom, J. (eds.), Developing Creativity in Higher Education: An Imaginative Curriculum, London and New York: Routledge, (pp. 1-9).

Kafai, Y. B. (2005) 'The classroom as "living laboratory": Design-based research for understanding, comparing, and evaluating learning science through design', Educational Technology, January/February, pp. 28–34.

McWilliam, E. (2007a) 'Is creativity teachable? Conceptualising the creativity/pedagogy relationship in higher education', 30th HERDSA Annual Conference: Enhancing higher education, theory and scholarship Proceedings, Adelaide: HERDSA.

McWilliam, E. (2007b) Developing pedagogical models for building creative workforce capacities in undergraduate students, Final Fellowship Report, Sydney: Australian Learning and Teaching Council.

McWilliam, E. and Haukka, S. (2008) 'Educating the creative workforce: new directions for twenty-first century schooling', British Educational Research Journal, vol. 34, no 5, pp. 651 - 666.

Naidu, S. (2004) 'Supporting learning with creative instructional designs', in Brindley, C. and Zawacki-Richter, O. (eds.), Learner Support in Open, Distance and Online Learning Environments, Oldenburg: Bibliotheks-und Informations system der Universitat Oldenburg, pp. 109-116.

Oliver, B. (2011) Good practice report: Assuring graduate outcomes, Canberra: Australian Learning and Teaching Council.

Pink, D. (2005) A whole new mind. Why right brainers will rule the future, New York: Riverhead.

Reeves, T., Herrington, J. and Oliver, R. (2005) 'Design research: A socially responsible approach to instructional technology research in higher education', Journal of Computing in Higher Education, vol. 16, no. 2, pp. 96-115.

Responding to the Australia 2020 Summit (2009) The Department of the Prime Minister and Cabinet, Australian Government, Canberra.

Robinson, K. (2001) Out of our minds: Learning to be creative, Oxford: Capstone Publishing.

The Design Based Research Collective (2003) 'Design-based research: An emerging paradigm for educational inquiry', Educational Researcher, vol. 32, no. 1, pp. 5-8.

The Global Creativity Corporation [Online], Available: http://www.globalcreativitycorp.com/ [12 Jan 2014].

Titus, P. A. (2000) 'Marketing and the creative problem-solving process', Journal of Marketing Education, vol. 22, no. 3, pp. 225-235.

Torrance, E. P. (1978). 'Developing creativity instructional materials according to the Osborn-Parnes Creative Problem Solving Model', Creative Child and Adult Quarterly, vol. 3, no. 2, pp. 80-90.

Tosey, P. (2006) 'Interfering with the interference: An emergent perspective on creativity in higher education', in Jackson, N., Oliver, M., Shaw and Wisdom, J., eds., Developing Creativity in Higher Education: An Imaginative Curriculum, Routledge, London, pp. 19-28.

Transforming Australia's higher education system (2009), Canberra: Common-wealth of Australia.

Vogt, S., A. Maschwitz and O. Zawacki-Richter (2010) 'From knowledge transfer to competence development – a case of learning by designing, World Conference on Educational Multimedia, Hypermedia and Telecommunications (EDMEDIA) 2010 Proceedings, Toronto, Canada: AACE.

Wood, D. (2010) 'Transforming the first-year learning experience through research based media practice', International Journal of First Year in Higher Education, vol. 1, no. 1, pp. 31-42.

Wood, D. & Bilsborow, C. (2013) 'Enhancing creative problem solving in the higher education curriculum through the use of innovative e-learning technologies', 8th International Conference on e-Learning ICEL-2013 Proceedings, 27-28 June, 2013, Cape Town, South Africa, pp. 416--423.

Wood, D., Lindsay, N., Corso, R., Gluth, S. and Bilsborow, C. (2011) 'Facilitating creative problem solving in the marketing curriculum in response to the demands of the networked information society', 15th World Marketing Congress Proceedings, Reims, France.

Wood, D., Corso, R., M Gluth, S., Scutter, S., Lindsay, N. and Bilsborow, C. (2015) Design as a catalyst for engaging students in creative problem solving: Final report (ID11-2053), Sydney: Office for Learning and Teaching. Available: http://www.olt.gov.au/system/files/resources/ID11_2053_Wood_Report_2015_0.pdf

Mobile Learning: A Kaleidoscope

Marlena Kruger and Riana Bester
CTI Education Group, GHO, Johannesburg, South Africa
Originally published in EJEL (2014) Volume 12 Issue 1

Editorial commentary

In this chapter, Kruger and Bester present an educational setting that most universities will experience sooner or later: the replacement of textbooks by course materials in digital format particularly on digital tablets. The added value of the study is to consider the epistemological issue (Christensen, 2008) -which pedagogies should we implement? - rather than the logistic one - what we should do with the tablets?

C. Christensen, M.B. Horn, C.W. Johnson (2008), Disrupting Class, How Disruptive Innovation Will Change the Way the World Learns. McGraw-Hill books.

Abstract: CTI is an accredited private higher education institution (university) with the Council on Higher Education (CHE) in South Africa. Its head office is in Fourways, Johannesburg. CTI has 12 campuses nationwide and offers higher certificates and degrees in commerce and information technology. These BCom and BSc degrees were rolled out to all 12 campuses from January 2013. All first year students received 10" Samsung tablets with their textbooks and course materials in digital format. We've worked closely with all role-players to ensure that all pillars for successful implementation of the e-book tablet project are in place. Timeous completion and conversion of course materials and e-textbooks for the start of the academic year in 2013 took extra time and focus of a dedicated project manager and multi-disciplinary team members. Several aspects were focused on during the conceptual, preparation and planning phases in 2012 (phase 1). This phase included aspects such as the student pilot project to establish the most suitable tablet to procure for students and lecturers, upgrading of infrastructure on campuses, lecturer training and the development of support materials, guidelines and rules for user standards. Phase 2 started in January 2013 with the implementation of a de-sign-based research project which includes several planned interventions to ensure continuous development and support of lecturers and students with the focus on enhancing the academic experience of students. During this phase qualitative and quantitative methodologies were implemented and included the sharing of experi-ences using different digital media, tools and instruments to gather data from lec-turers, students and other role-players. Data was analysed and compared with different theoretical frameworks for using and integrating innovative technologies in learning environments. Changes that took place in teaching and learning prac-tices will be discussed by way of using the technology integration matrix and other measurements to determine the development and movement of teaching and learning practices towards emerging pedagogies for the information age. More detail of research methodologies, actions and interventions as well as data gather-ing methods during project will be focused on and shared in this article.

Keywords: mobile learning, e-textbooks, tablet computers, faculty development, students' enhancement of academic experience

1 Background: Discussion of research problem and motivation for study

Previously, CTI students received printed textbooks that were included in their fees. From 2013, new degree and higher certificate students are re-ceiving tablet computers with e-books instead of printed text books. This per se is not a problem but research on the use of tablet computers for teaching and learning is needed for various reasons. Firstly: Literature re-garding the use of tablet computers in higher education is limited to publi-cations that report on using it as e book readers. In the second place does very little evidence exist of research that investigated a project of this ex-tent specifically in *higher education in South Africa*. The third reason for more research is that most of the educational applications available for the use on tablet computers are focused on primary and secondary learners.

At CTI, a research project was started in January 2013, to identify the criti-cal issues that will influence the optimum utilisation of tablets and e-books to improve the quality of teaching, learning and assessment. The focus of this paper is on one of three perspectives that were investigated in a re-search project at CTI, namely the lecturers' perspective. The other two perspectives, which include that of the students and the infrastructure, will be briefly discussed and referred to where relevant.

1.1 Problem statement

Challenges for *lecturers* who used tablets during the first semester of 2013 at CTI include the following:

- Tablet computers, like other technologies, have the potential to become a distraction to students in class if it is not applied for structured activities.
- Additional to this, a high percentage of CTI's lecturers have never used a tablet computer for teaching, learning and assessment and some lecturers have never used a tablet computer at all.

Issues experienced by CTI's *students* include that

- Many of our students come from communities where not only in-frastructure like wireless networks often does not exist but basic resources like electricity is also not a given.
- Technology has not been implemented in all schools and many students did not have exposure to the use of technology for teaching, learning and assessment.

These problems lead to our research question:
"What are the principles (critical issues) for the optimum utilisation of tab-lets and e-books to improve the quality of teaching, learning and assess-ment in a private higher education institution in South Africa?"

1.2 Aims and objectives of the study

The research problem discussed, as well as the research question that was stated above determines that aim of this research project should be to identify principles for the optimum utilisation of tablets and e-books to improve the quality of teaching, learning and assessment in a private higher education institution *in South Africa.*

To achieve this aim the following objectives were formulated, from three perspectives:

1.2.1 Lecturer perspective

To provide iterative cycles of collaborative learning opportunities for lec-turers in order to guide them through stages of acquisition, participation and contribution and eventually transformative (improved) practice (Stetsenko, 2008).

- To gather evidence that will demonstrate how lecturers integrate technology in the classroom regarding
  - o Approaches/strategies that they apply
  - o Methods that they employ
  - o Specific technologies/applications that they use
- To subsequently identify principles of best practice of using tablets for teaching, learning and assessment, in other words to identify models of best practice, and record 'lessons learnt'

1.2.2 *Student perspective*
- To investigate the impact of the use of tablets and e-books on teaching, learning and assessment
- To investigate the impact of the use of tablets on "changing the digital difference" and equipping students with additional skills
- To conduct a practical, usability study from the students' perspective

1.2.3 *Institutional (CTI) perspective*
- To monitor and timeously identify problem areas
- To describe and adjust the infrastructure on campuses according to the needs of all users

This paper will concentrate on the first perspective, namely that of the lecturers.

2 Literature review and theoretical framework

Marc Prensky (2001) started a *generational* debate about the use of Information and Communication Technologies (ICTs) in education, early in the new millennium. He implied a generational *division* in this regard when he named young people who use digital technology with confidence because they grew up with it, "digital natives" and older, "more mature" users of technology, "digital immigrants". Prensky alleged that the digital native generation have different expectations of life in general, and also specifically of learning.

Although this information is helpful it regrettably led to sweeping statements about digital natives such as *"...they are forcing a change in the model of pedagogy..."* (Tapscott, 2009). This is presently the cause of needlessly high levels of distress amongst many educators who often fear that learners might not respect them because of their lesser experience with technology. Some educators feel *bewildered* about the influence that technology might have on learning (Palfrey & Gasser quoted in Jones) and some even seem to be in a state of *"moral panic"* (Bennet, Maton, & Kervin, 2008). However, there is no clear-cut proof that young students *intentionally* form generational cohorts or express *generation* based demands pertaining to the use of technology for their studies (Jones & Binhui, 2011). Students who commence higher education, do not all possess the same level of technology proficiency (Nakamaru, 2011) and therefore do not belong to a single, homogeneous digital generation (Jones & Binhui, 2011). Furthermore, can the *diversity* of technology users not solely be ascribed to a difference in age; demographic factors play an equally important role (Jones & Binhui, 2011). This is especially relevant in the South-African context. Although a "digital difference" might exist between educators and learners it is fortunately not rigid or impossible to overcome (Jones & Binhui, 2011).

Almost a decade after he introduced the *"digital native and immigrant"* idea, Prensky introduced a *new* concept, namely that of *"digital wisdom"* (Prensky, 2009). He *now* proposed that everyone can become a *"digitally enhanced individual"* with digital wisdom obtainable through sufficient engagement with technology. This should reassure the older generation of educators but it also obliges them to attain digital wisdom for the sake of their learners, since technology has become an essential part of human development (Jones & Binhui, 2011). Related to Prensky's ideas is Stoerger's (2009) metaphor, the "Digital Melting Pot". It describes the *variety* of technological aptitude and the *co-existence* of today's technology users effectively. This also emphasises the *opportunities for participation* during which less competent technology users can become transformed through their own interaction with technology, as well as by the contributions of peers and other more experienced individuals (Stetsenko, 2008). Educators should be brave and humble enough to be lifelong learners and accept to learn not only with their learners(students) but also from them!

Educators should therefore make the most of technology as a mediational tool for teaching and learning and not simply dismiss it as a distraction. This will nonetheless only be possible if the integration of technology in the curriculum is well informed in order to promote *meaningful* learning. A more detailed and structured description for this melting pot of technology mediated doings is provided by Engeström's (Engeström, 2009) notion of an activity system depicted in Figure 2. This idea of Engeström was derived from Vygotsky's "Mediation triangle" and both these concepts are anchored in the Cultural Historical Activity Theory (CHAT), which is the theoretical framework of this study. According to Vygotsky, human action is object orientated and artefact (tool) mediated. His original notion of mediation is illustrated in Figure 1.

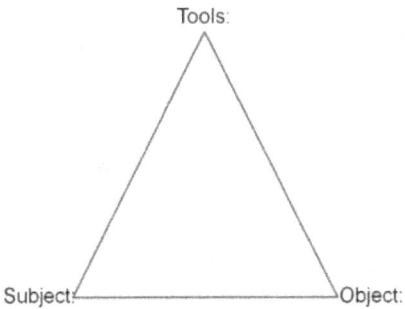

Figure 1: Vygotsky's mediation triangle   Figure 2: Engeström's activity system

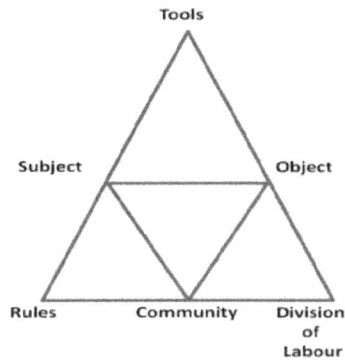

In spite of its simple structure, this diagram not only indicates the relationship between three central elements of human action: subject, instrument, and object (Engeström, Miettinen, & Punamäki, 1999), but also exemplifies the importance of tools in the mediation process as well as the fact that human action is always purposeful and directed at achieving a specific goal. Lautenbach (2005) described activity as human doings that work towards a common goal by employing *internal or external tools*, in order to reach a desired outcome. He (Lautenbach, 2011b) also stated that educational technologies can provide and support interventions by extending the human mediating presence.

However, Vygotsky's triangle does not explain this role that other humans play during activity. For this reason Engeström extended Vygotsky triangle to include another three elements; the community, its associated rules as well as the division of labour that is a result of diversity. Although this system is more complex, it is more applicable when focusing on the integration and use of technologies in the learning environment.

3   Research design and methodology

A mixed method (qualitative as well as quantitative) research approach was followed to gather data for the lecturer perspective i.e. to identify principles for the optimum implementation of tablet computers and e-books by lecturers, to improve their learning facilitation. A Design-based Research (DBR) design is most appropriate for the CTI educational context. This research design is seen as a "socially responsible" design for educational research (Reeves, Herrington, & Oliver, 2005) and we believe it to be in line with the vision of ICEL to bring together, as well as gain understanding of academic research *and* proven best practices. Another reason for our choice of methodology is that an activity system is normally used as unit of analysis during Design-based research (Engeström, 2009). The origin and concept of an extended activity system as part of CHAT was already explained during the literature review (Lautenbach, 2011).

3.1   Design-based research

Various alternative terms are often used for this mostly qualitative research design; "design experiment", "design research" and "development research". The purpose of this research approach is to develop *solutions* to educational *challenges* in naturalistic learning situations and entails the implementation of practical interventions.

These interventions should never randomly be put into practice, but should always be anchored in theory, carefully planned and adhering to the following criteria:

Design-based Research is:

- Theory-driven; testing theoretical suppositions, which guide the design of interventions
- Interventionist; includes not only designed learning settings but also the systematic investigation of expected relationship between aspects of the intervention on learning
- Process-focused; trying to comprehend both the learning process and the influence of the designed interventions on that learning.
- Utility oriented; aiming to produce practical knowledge for educational improvement
- Collaborative; knowledge is constructed through participation and contribution of both the researcher and the participants
- Iterative; consisting of repeated cycles of planning, acting, observing and reflecting. Each cycle will consist of four distinctive, yet overlapping phases of planning, acting, observing and reflecting. Cycles will follow and build on each other as illustrated in Figure 4 (Adapted from (Rhodes, 2012) that follows.

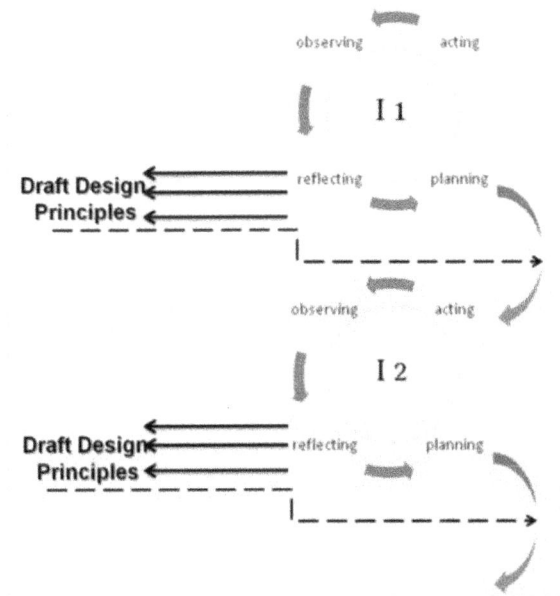

Figure 3: Successive learning interventions

Our study, and the planned series of interventions (PSI) will be based on this model. Each intervention cycle will be *planned* by the researcher as a collaborative learning opportunity, providing suggestions of applications, methods and strategies to use on the tablet. Activities will be planned to include those that are active, collaborative, creative, integrative as well as evaluative, concentrating on developing a new pedagogy that is appropriate for the information age and not just adapt existing traditional pedagogies for the sake of using technology (See Table 1).

Table 1: Classroom practice using emerging pedagogy for information age

Aspect	Less of *"Traditional Pedagogy"*	More of *"Emerging Pedagogy for information age"*
Active	Activities prescribed by teachers	Activities determined through negotiation
	Whole-class instruction	Small groups
	Little variation activities	Varied activities
	Pace determined by program	Pace determined by students
Collaboration	Individual	Working in teams
	Homogeneous groups	Heterogeneous groups
	Everyone for her/himself	Supporting each other
Creative	Reproductive learning	Productive learning
	Apply known solutions to problems	Find new solutions for problems
Integrative	No link between theory and practice	Integrating theory and practice
	Separate subjects	Relations between subjects
	Discipline based	Theme based
	Individual teaching	Teams of teachers or lecturers
Evaluative	Teacher or lecturer directed	Student directed
	Summative	Formative

Using this strategy to assist lecturers should encourage them to start transforming their learning facilitation (teaching) as well. During the *"acting"* phase lecturers will be requested to participate in the learning activities to acquire new knowledge and skills. Support will be available at all times. During the *"observing"* phase participants will be encouraged to contribute by providing suggestions of their own. The *"reflection"* phase will guide the planning of subsequent interventions. During this phase the researcher will identify preliminary principles for the optimal utilisation of tablets for teaching, learning and assessment. These principles will be the result of combined efforts by the researcher and the participants and can be included or adapted for subsequent phases.

4 Actions and timeframes

The following learning opportunities/interventions **were planned** (see tables)

- For November 2012:
  - ○ A first learning intervention in the form of face-to-face tablet and e-book training workshops was *planned*, presented *("acted out")* and *observed* on all 12 CTI campuses. Feedback was requested in the form of a survey.

- For the first semester of 2013:

  - ○ An "online learning space" to build a community of practice
  - ○ A "Research and Development Seminar" (RDS) on each campus to identify champions
  - ○ One central "Research Indaba" (RI) where selected lecturers (champions) from all campuses will report and share their progress and learn from each other's experiences.
- For the second semester of 2013:

  - ○ A continuation of electronic learning interventions and community of practice
  - ○ A second RDS on each campus to identify champions during November.

The following interventions have already taken place:

4.1 Intervention 1:

Tablet and e-book orientation workshops were conducted in November and December 2012 on all 12 of CTI's campuses. The lecturers received their tablets as well as hard copies of support manuals at these face-to-face and "hands-on" sessions. About 100 lecturers attended these workshops. After these workshops, in January 2013, a questionnaire was sent out to lecturers to evaluate their attitudes towards the use of tablets before and after the training as well as after the holidays. Thirty-seven lecturers completed and returned the questionnaire. The results obtained from this questionnaire indicated that the majority of the lecturers felt more positive after the training than before.

4.2 Intervention 2:

In February 2013, an online community was created on Google Groups to provide learning and collaboration opportunities for lecturers. Three learning tasks were posted.

- The purpose of the first learning task, namely to post a collage of themselves, was to encourage lecturers to introduce themselves on this platform, in order to nurture a culture of collaboration and develop this group as a community of practice (COP). Additional, this activity introduced those that have never used a platform such as Google Groups, to the basic functions of it.
- The second learning task on Google Groups firstly aimed to introduce the lecturers to the Technology Integration Matrix (TIM), depicted in Table 1, as a theoretical framework for their teaching with technology. It secondly served as an evaluation tool to choose appropriate technologies for teaching and learning with the help of the tablets. The lecturers were requested to evaluate "Socrative", an assessment tool, as well as another application of their own choice with the TIM. Table 2 provides an example of how the TIM can be used to evaluate technologies as mediating tools.
- The third learning task continued on the foundation laid by the second, where the lecturers were requested to plan a specific lesson or a short series of lessons and indicate which platforms and applications they would use to utilise the tablets in a blended learning approach. They were asked to choose resources with the TIM in mind.

Table 2: Technology Integration Matrix

Characteristics of Learning environment	Level of Technology Integration into the Curriculum →				
	1	2	3	4	5
a. **Active:** Students are actively engaged in using technology as a tool rather than passively receiving information from the technology.	Students mainly use technology for **drill and practice** and computer based training.	Students are beginning to utilize prescribed technology tools to **create products, according to specific criteria**, for example use a word processor to create a report.	Students are provided with opportunities to **modify or personalise the use of pre-scribed tech-nology tools to** accomplish purposes, for example use colour or add graphics to MS office documents	Students are empowered and encouraged through-out the day to **select appro-priate tech-nology tools** and actively apply them to the tasks at hand.	Students are provided with ongoing access to online re-sources, and encouraged to actively select and pursue topics **beyond the limitations of the re-source cen-tre**
b. **Collabora-tive:** Students use technology tools to collabo-rate with others rather than working indi-vidually at all times.	Students primarily work **alone** when using technology.	Opportunities are provided for students to utilize pre-scribed col-laborative tools, such as email, in **con-ventional ways**.	Students are allowed to select and **modify technology tools to facilitate** collaborative work.	Opportunities are created for students throughout the day and across sub-ject areas, to utilize technol-ogy tools to facilitate col-laborative learning.	Opportunities are created for students to use tech-nology that enable them to **collabo-rate with peers and experts irrespective of time zone or physical distances.**
c. **Construc-tive:** Students use technology tools to build understanding rather than simply receive information.	Technology is **only** used to **deliver information** to students.	Students are encouraged to utilize pre-**scribed con-structive tools** such as graphic organ-izers to build upon prior knowledge and construct meaning.	Opportunities are created and students are allowed to select and **modify technology tools to assist** them in the con-struction of un-derstanding.	Students are allowed and opportunities are created for them to utilize technology to make connec-tions and con-struct under-standing **across disci-plines** and throughout the day.	Students are allowed and opportunities are created for them to utilize tech-nology to construct, share, and publish knowledge to a worldwide audience.

Characteristics of Learning environment	Level of Technology Integration into the Curriculum →				
	1	2	3	4	5
d. <u>Authentic</u>: Students use technology tools to solve real-world problems meaningful to them rather than working on artificial assignments.	Students are **only** expected to use technology to complete assigned activities that are **generally unrelated** to real-world problems.	Students are provided with opportunities to apply technology tools to complete **some content-specific activities that are** based on real-world problems.	Students are provided with opportunities to select and modify technology tools to solve problems based on real-**world** issues that are not necessarily content specific.	Students are allowed to select appropriate technology tools to complete authentic tasks across disciplines.	By means of technology tools, students are encouraged to participate in **outside-of-school projects** and problem-solving activities that have **meaning for the students and the community.**
e. <u>Goal Directed</u>: Students use technology tools to set goals, plan activities, monitor progress, and evaluate results rather than simply completing assignments without reflection.	Students are **provided with directions, guidance, and feedback** from technology, rather than using technology tools to set goals, plan activities, monitor progress, or self-evaluate.	From time to time, students are provided with opportunities to **use technology to either plan, monitor, or evaluate an activity.**	Students are provided with opportunities to **select and modify the use of technology tools** to facilitate goal-setting, planning, monitoring, and evaluating specific activities.	Students are provided with opportunities to use technology tools to set goals, plan activities, monitor progress, and evaluate results throughout the curriculum.	Students are **guided to engage in ongoing metacognitive activities** at a level that would be unattainable without the support of technology tools.

120

Table 3: Evaluation of applications with the Technology Integration Matrix

Characteristics of Learning environment ↓ ↓ ↓	Level of Technology Integration into the Curriculum → → →				
	1	2	3	4	5
a. Active				X	
b. Collaborative			X		
c. Constructive		X			
d. Authentic		X			
e. Goal Directed			X		

4.3   Interventions 3 and 4:

In May and June of this year, Research and Development Seminars (RDSs) were conducted at each of CTI's 12 campuses. In addition, a national Research Indaba (RI) was held in Johannesburg at the end of June. During these events, lecturers had the opportunity to report on their experiences with tablets and e-books during the first semester of 2013. Lecturers were asked to convey what they did, what worked, what did not work as well as to make recommendations for the future implementation of technology in teaching, learning and assessment at CTI. Their presentations were observed and evaluated. 44 lecturers reported at the RDSs and 24 of these again at the RI. During a qualitative analysis of the data (observation of presentations and document analysis of 44 PowerPoint presentations), the most important issues (categories) were identified.

To triangulate this qualitative data and enhance the reliability and validity thereof, a questionnaire with 38 questions – based on the identified issues – was compiled and distributed to all lecturers who received tablets during the first semester of 2013. A total of 69 questionnaires were received back between 11 and 19 July 2013 and was subsequently analysed. This number of 69 represents 53% of the 130 lecturers who received tablets. The next section includes an analysis and graphical comparisons between the qualitative and quantitative data.

4.4   Intervention 5:

During the second semester (July – October 2013), a second extended electronic learning intervention using another online space, namely "Edmodo" was initiated and monitored. The first objective was yet again to build and strengthen the community of practice between participating lecturers across time and distance that separate CTI's 12 campuses. The second objective was to introduce the use of a learning management system. We hoped that newcomers would be inspired to participate after observing the feedback of the 'more experienced' lecturers that already participated during the interventions of the first semester.

Edmodo was chosen for several reasons. Lecturers can (and should) invite students to join the classrooms that they create. Edmodo can be used to communicate with their students, share information, post assignments and perform assessments. Other lecturers can also join as "observing teachers" and can therefore benefit not only by means of their own participation but also by observing that of other lecturers. Lecturers ("Teachers" on Edmodo) can join communities. The difference between the electronic learning intervention of the first semester and this was that students can be included and their participation observed. Again three learning tasks were given to the lecturers.

A qualitative analysis of lecturers' reflection diaries still needs to be completed.

5   Findings and data analysis

5.1   Data collection methods and instruments

As previously discussed, Design-based Research requires a mixed method approach because qualitative as well as supporting quantitative data is needed. Therefore a variety of instruments were be utilised.

5.1.1   Questionnaires

Two different questionnaires were used, to obtain three different data sets, as discussed in the previous section:
- To obtain biographical data of students and lecturers.

- To obtain qualitative data of lecturers' first experience (feelings/attitudes) with tablets as well as the training workshops
- To determine the progress and level of integration of technology according to the "Technology Integration Matrix"

5.1.2   Document analysis
Online resources like e-mails, participation on the electronic platform and PowerPoint presentations will be analysed.

5.1.3   Evaluation forms
Evaluation forms of lecturers' presentations at the Research and Development seminars that will be hosted on all twelve campuses. These forms will be completed by peers (other lecturers), principals and academic coordinators.

5.2   Findings of intervention 1
These findings were obtained from the first questionnaire. This sample of participants consisted of lectures that responded by completing the questionnaire and represents 32% of the total of the lecturers that attended the training.

The first section of questions aimed to collect biographical information regarding the lecturers and include age, gender and subject area.
The age distribution of the sample of the participating lecturers is shown below in Figure 4.

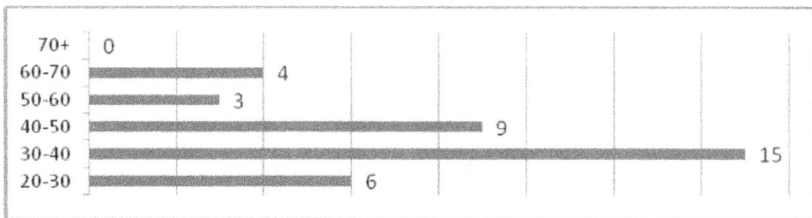

Figure 4: Age of sample of participating lecturers

Of the sample 14 participants were female and 23 male

Of the sample 12 participants are IT lecturers, 24 are Business lecturers and 1 person teaches in both fields of study

The second section of questions was aimed at collecting data regarding the use of technology by the lecturers

Only 4 of the 37 participants indicated that they have never used computers for teaching purposes before

15 lecturers have used tablets before and 22 have not

10 of the 15 lecturers who used tablets previously, used Samsung tablets

The third and last section of the questionnaire included open ended questions, to determine the attitudes of the lecturers towards the use of tablet computers *before and after* the training workshops. The results are depicted below in Figure 5.

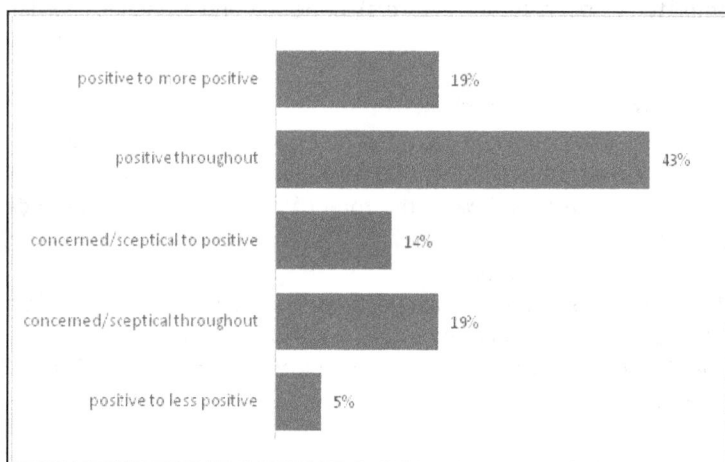

Figure 5: Attitude changes of lecturers before and after training workshops - Percentage

5.3   Findings of intervention 2

The lecturers who attended the campus RDSs and the RI were asked to answer the following four open-ended questions during their presentations:

1. What did you do?
2. What worked?
3. What did not work?
4. What do you recommend now?

In this section, qualitative as well as quantitative findings will be presented – mainly in the form of graphs – and then analysed, interpreted and discussed.

5.3.1 What did they do?

Lecturers had the opportunity to report on what they did during the first semester even before the RDS and RI. All lecturers who received tablets were invited to join the COP, which was created on "Google Groups" in February. They were requested to participate in four Learning Tasks during the course of the first semester. These were described in paragraph 1.3: Intervention 2. Lecturers were also encouraged to share information and ask advice from other group members. An analysis of the 84 posts on Google Groups showed that the lecturers used this platform as shown in Figure 6.

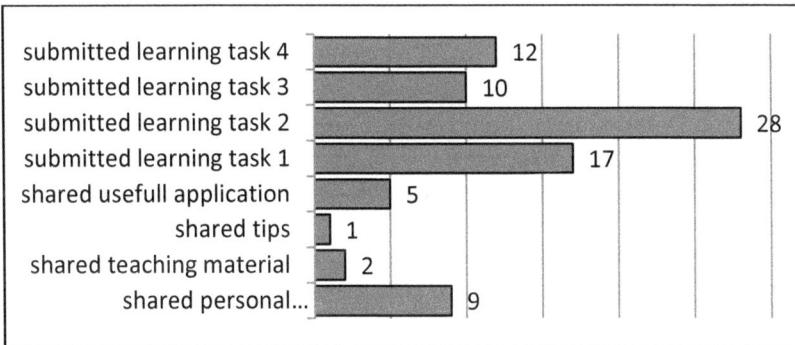

Figure 6: Lecturer activities on COP in first semester – "What did you do?"

This chart indicates that lecturers used the COP mainly to submit their Learning Tasks (50 of the 84 posts). However, during the RDSs, several lecturers reported that although they did not participate in the COP, they observed the activities of the group members, and benefitted from it ("lurked"). These lecturers also remarked that their non-participation was mainly due to a lack of time.

During the RDSs, all lecturers reported back on how they accessed and used the e-books (CTI course books and Pearson eText) as well as other applications. These applications are:

- Cite me
- Droid edit
- Dropbox
- E planner
- Ebscohost
- Edmodo
- End note
- English dictionary offline
- Evernote
- Facebook
- Freebookcentre.net
- G talk

- WhatsApp
- Google drive
- HR exec magazine
- HR management
- HR tools
- Khan academy
- Kingsoft Office
- Linkedin
- Mind tools
- Online personality tests
- Socrative

5.3.2 What worked?

The lecturer presentations from the RDSs and RI yielded valuable qualitative data. After having analysed this data, various themes were identified. These themes can be arranged into the following **four** categories:
1. On-campus infrastructure
2. Device-specific issues/requirements/preferences
3. Software-specific issues/requirements/preferences
4. Implications for teaching and learning

The identified problems were addressed in the questionnaire to determine the opinions of a bigger sample of lecturers.

At this point, it is necessary to stress that the charts representing the qualitative data (derived from the lecturer presentations) should at all times be read and interpreted in conjunction with the related charts representing the quantitative data obtained from the questionnaire.

Maggie Hutchings, Anne Qunney and Kate Galvin

Qualitative data obtained from the analysis of lecturer presentations

The following graph in Figure 7 represents the variety of themes mentioned by lecturers during presentations at the RDSs and RI.

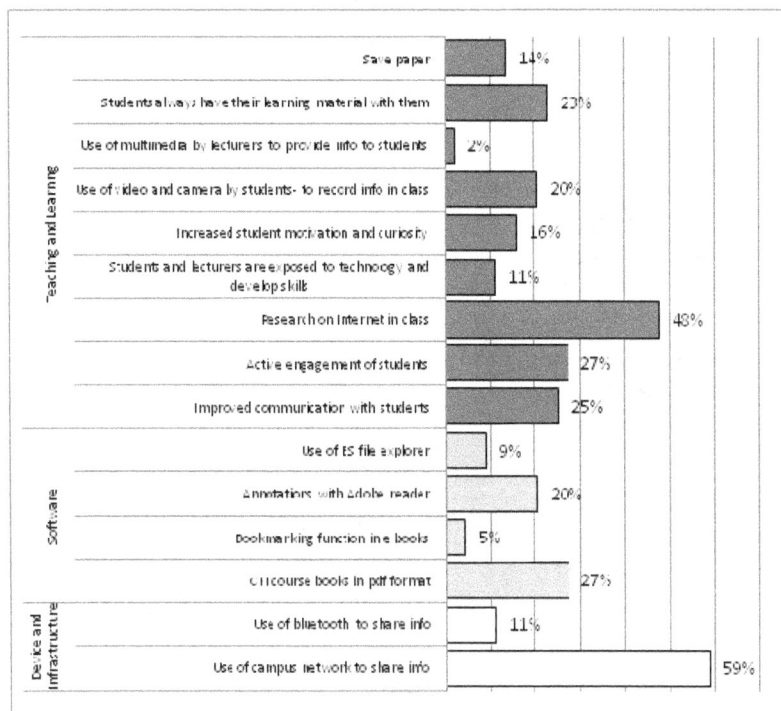

Figure 7: Qualitative data - "What worked?"

The aspect that lecturers reported most favourably on (59% of lecturers
mentioned it) was the convenience and ease of sharing information with
their students on the campus network. Related to this was lecturer satisfaction with the CTI course books that were also available on the campus
network. Another very prominent, positive aspect was that the majority of
lecturers agreed that the use of tablets and e-books enhances teaching and
learning. A substantial proportion of the lecturers (27%) were of the opinion that tablets encourage the active engagement of students, and an even
larger proportion (48%) were more specific and mentioned that the tablets
enable students to do online research in class. For this reason, a set of

questions addressing the remaining four aspects of the TIM was included in the questionnaire.

Quantitative data obtained from the lecturer questionnaire
Questions relating to the TIM (refer to paragraph 1.3, Intervention 2) were included in the questionnaire because the TIM was used as a theoretical framework for the learning tasks completed by the lecturers during the first semester. The TIM was also used as a tool for reflection with which lecturers could evaluate the different elements of their own teaching and learning practices. The majority of the lecturers agreed or fully agreed that the use of tablets promotes transformative teaching and learning practices because it fosters active engagement, collaboration as well as constructive, authentic and goal-directed learning. This is shown in Figure 8.

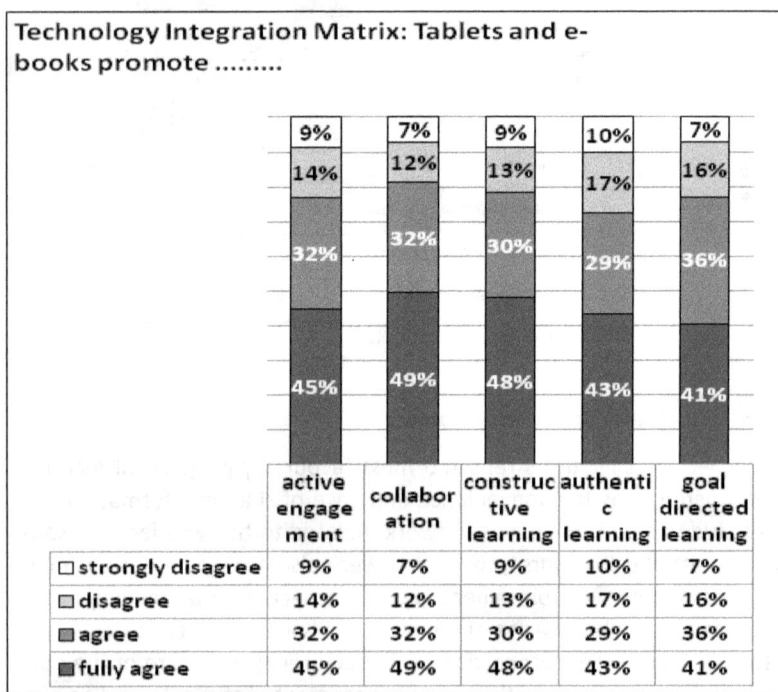

Technology Integration Matrix: Tablets and e-books promote ....

	active engagement	collaboration	constructive learning	authentic learning	goal directed learning
☐ strongly disagree	9%	7%	9%	10%	7%
☐ disagree	14%	12%	13%	17%	16%
▣ agree	32%	32%	30%	29%	36%
■ fully agree	45%	49%	48%	43%	41%

Figure 8: Benefits of tablets and e-books for teaching and learning according to TIM

There were a number of *other* related topics that emerged from the presentations that indicated that lecturers believe that the use of tablets augments teaching and learning. These topics were specifically addressed in the questionnaire and yielded the results shown in Figure 9.

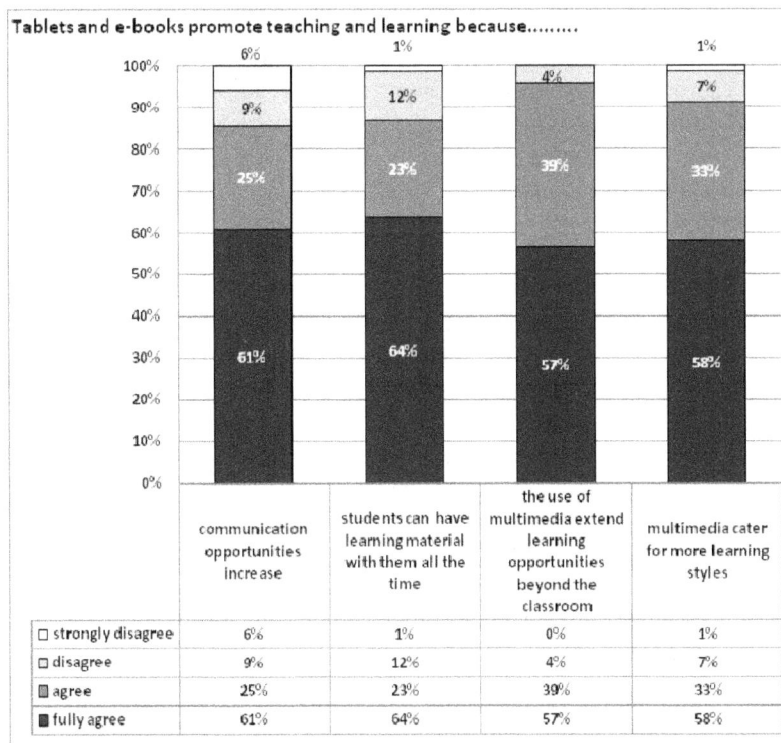

Tablets and e-books promote teaching and learning because.........

	communication opportunities increase	students can have learning material with them all the time	the use of multimedia extend learning opportunities beyond the classroom	multimedia cater for more learning styles
☐ strongly disagree	6%	1%	0%	1%
☐ disagree	9%	12%	4%	7%
▨ agree	25%	23%	39%	33%
■ fully agree	61%	64%	57%	58%

Figure 9: Other benefits of tablets and e-books for teaching and learning

The most important insight from this section ("What worked?") is therefore that lecturers feel that the use of tablets can help improve the quality of teaching and learning as well as promote transformative teaching practices.

5.3.3   What did not work?

Qualitative data obtained from the analysis of lecturer presentations
Note: Please remember to interpret the qualitative data in conjunction with the related quantitative data.

The analysis of the lecturer presentations provided valuable qualitative data regarding the nature of problems experienced on the various campuses. These problems were divided into the following four categories:

- On-campus infrastructure
- Device-specific issues
- Software-specific issues
- Implications for teaching and learning

The information gleaned from the lecturer presentations was used to compile the questionnaire where the above categories of problems were addressed by means of more specific questions. The opinions of a bigger sample of lecturers could therefore be obtained in the form of quantitative data. Figure 10 represents the problems mentioned by lecturers during their presentations at the RDSs and the RI.

The insufficient Wi-Fi coverage on the campuses was by far the most prevalent cause of frustration for lecturers (64% mentioned this). Following on this were the problems encountered with the Pearson eText application (32%) and the students' inability to use technology (23%).

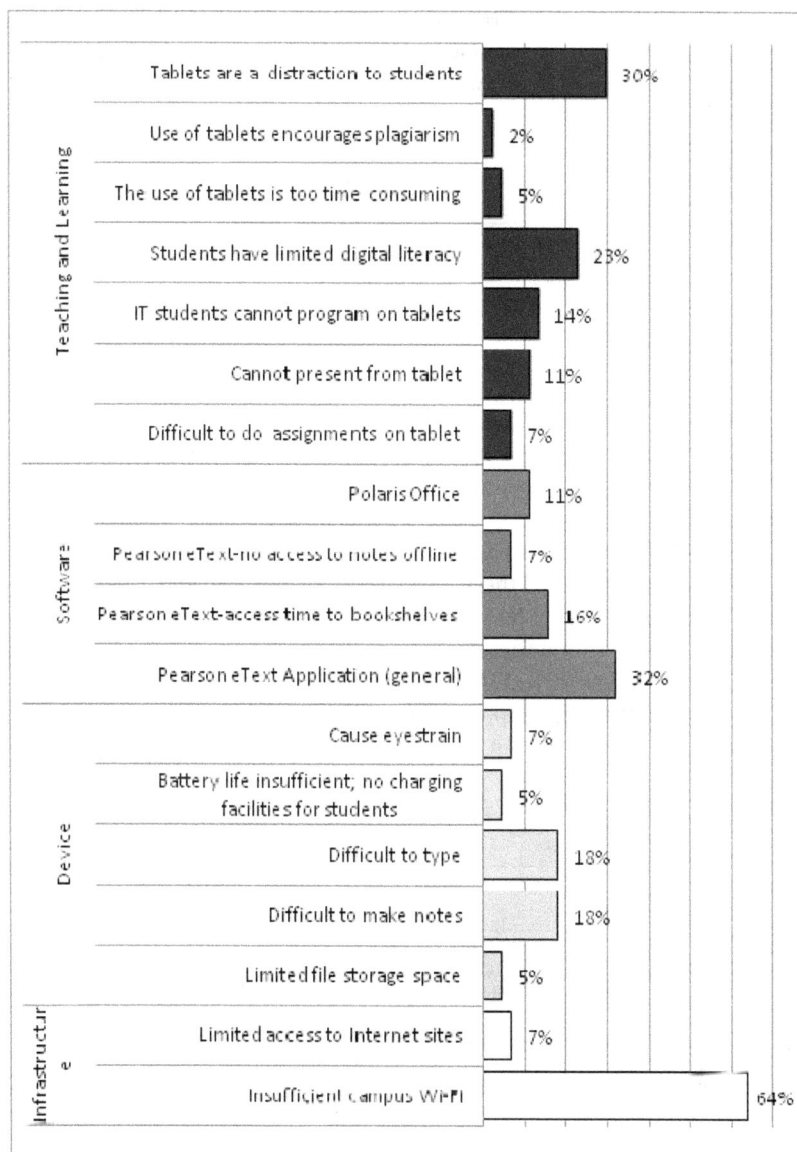

Teaching and Learning

Tablets are a distraction to students	30%
Use of tablets encourages plagiarism	2%
The use of tablets is too time consuming	5%
Students have limited digital literacy	23%
IT students cannot program on tablets	14%
Cannot present from tablet	11%
Difficult to do assignments on tablet	7%

Software

Polaris Office	11%
Pearson eText-no access to notes offline	7%
Pearson eText-access time to bookshelves	16%
Pearson eText Application (general)	32%

Device

Cause eyestrain	7%
Battery life insufficient; no charging facilities for students	5%
Difficult to type	18%
Difficult to make notes	18%
Limited file storage space	5%

Infrastructure

Limited access to Internet sites	7%
Insufficient campus WiFi	64%

Figure 10: Qualitative data: "What did not work?"

Quantitative data obtained from the lecturer questionnaire

The majority of lecturers, namely 48 of the 69 (69%), described the Wi-Fi coverage as insufficient or unsatisfactory as shown in Figure 11.

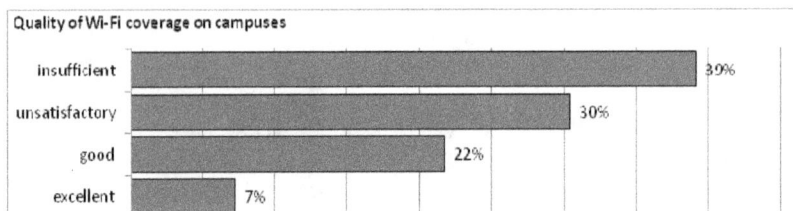

Quality of Wi-Fi coverage on campuses

insufficient	39%
unsatisfactory	30%
good	22%
excellent	7%

Figure 11: Quality of Wi-Fi coverage on campuses

The remaining 29% of lecturers that indicated otherwise might be lecturers who were lucky enough to have good Wi-Fi coverage in their classes and offices. During the RDSs, lecturers reported that Wi-Fi coverage was either generally bad or only good in certain areas on a campus. A few lecturers remarked during the presentations how students soon identified the "good" areas and gathered there, often on staircases and in the passages.

40 of the 69 lecturers (58%) who completed the questionnaire had used Pearson eText books and therefore the Pearson eText application (see Figure 7). Thirty of these 40 lecturers, therefore 75%, who used Pearson eText books indicated that they experienced problems with the eText application (see Figure 8). The breakdown of e-book usage can be seen in Figure 12.

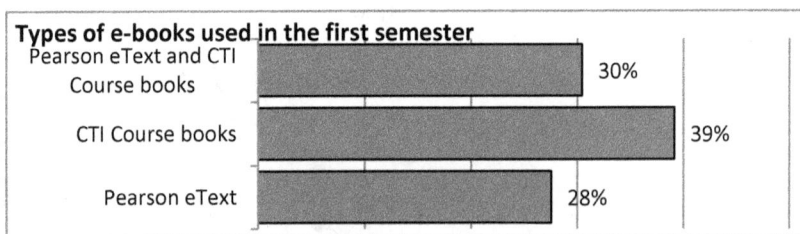

Types of e-books used in the first semester

Pearson eText and CTI Course books	30%
CTI Course books	39%
Pearson eText	28%

Figure 12: Types of e-books used in the first semester

Several lecturers indicated that they experienced problems with some of the standard applications on the tablets. This matter therefore seemed worth investigating with specific questions in the questionnaire.

Maggie Hutchings, Anne Qunney and Kate Galvin

A comparison of the problems experienced with the applications revealed the following results (see figure 13): most of the problems experienced by lecturers, excluding those experienced with Pearson eText, were with CTI course books and the distribution of material via the campus networks. This seemed to be directly related to the Wi-Fi coverage and campus infrastructure. One other application that caused frustration was "Polaris Office", one of the standard applications on the Samsung Galaxy tablet. A substantial number of lecturers suggested that the "Kingsoft Office" application be used instead. It will therefore be tested in the second semester and recommendations will be made accordingly. It is possible that the problems experienced with ES File Explorer occurred when lecturers tried to up- or download material to or from the campus networks. Ten per cent of lecturers experienced problems with Adobe Reader, a situation that can be resolved by using this software more often.

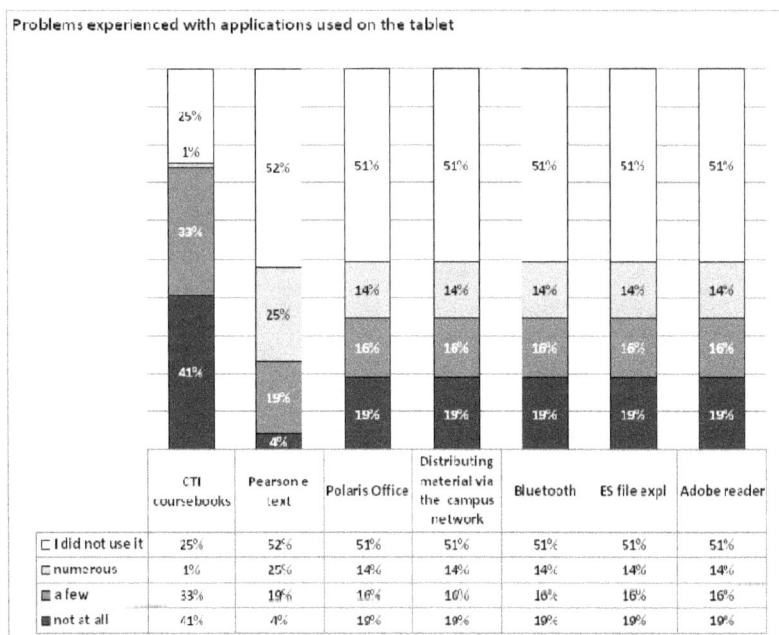

Problems experienced with applications used on the tablet

	CTI coursebooks	Pearson e text	Polaris Office	Distributing material via the campus network	Bluetooth	ES file expl	Adobe reader
I did not use it	25%	52%	51%	51%	51%	51%	51%
numerous	1%	25%	14%	14%	14%	14%	14%
a few	33%	19%	16%	16%	16%	16%	16%
not at all	41%	4%	19%	19%	19%	19%	19%

Figure 13: Problems experienced with applications used on the tablet

133

The concerns of lecturers who participated in the RDSs and the RI regarding students' lack of digital literacy were reiterated in their answers to a specific question in the questionnaire addressing this problem (see Figure 14).

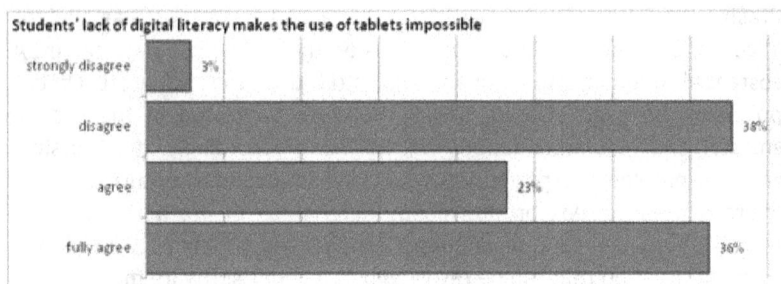

Figure 14: Students' lack of digital literacy makes the use of tablets impossible

411 of the 69 lecturers agreed or fully agreed that this makes the use of tablets for teaching and learning impossible. This amounts to 60% of the lecturers who completed the questionnaire. A change in the format and frequency of the training for students might alleviate the problem and alter this opinion. Student training and support, as well as the planned involvement of resource centre staff in this regard, will be discussed in the following section.

5.3.4   Recommendations made by lecturers

Qualitative data obtained from observations and document analysis of lecturer presentations
Note: Please remember to interpret the qualitative data in conjunction with the related quantitative data.

Figure 15 denotes the various themes of recommendations made by lecturers during their presentations at the RDSs and the RI. The recommendation most often made by lecturers was that to upgrade the campuses' Wi-Fi networks came out the strongest. The second group of most common suggestions recommendation related to student training. The third recommendation was that a **Learning Management System (LMS)** be implemented to support blended learning was the third important need that

134

was identified. The fourth aspect that needs consideration, implied by several requests that were made, was for either a different **device** or added functionalities to the device that is currently being used. These four recommendations obtained by the qualitative data analysis were further investigated and confirmed by means of specific questions in the questionnaire (see figures 15-19).

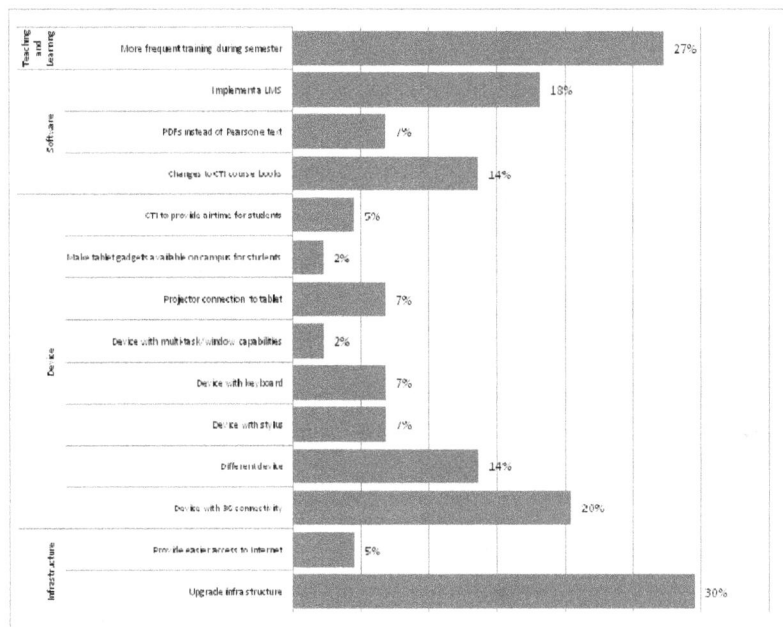

Figure 15: Qualitative data: Recommendations made by lecturers

Quantitative data obtained from the lecturer questionnaire

Answers to the questions pertaining to the format of future training for lecturers as well as students (see Figure 11) indicated not only that lecturers feel the face face-to to-face element should not be completely removed but also and that an electronic component should be added to provide a blended learning approach and on-going accessibility to training material and learning opportunities.

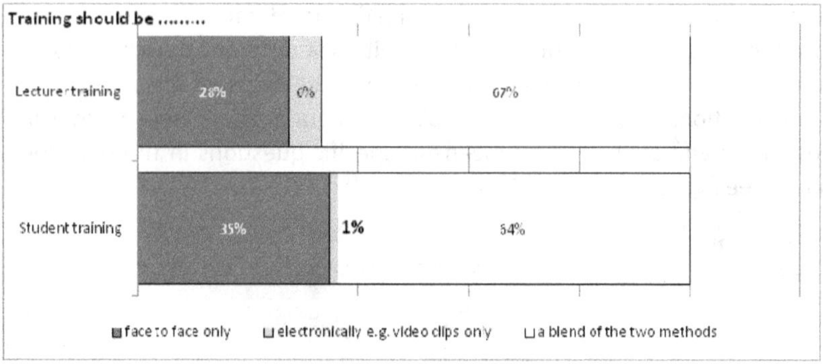

Figure 16: Requested format of training

The need to change the format and frequency of training for students exists because students are allowed to register late in the semester and they receive their tablets only once payment for their studies has been finalised. As a result, many students attended the training without devices and could not use it when they received it as late as March in certain cases. Students admitted in the mid-year intake in July might have similar experiences. The inclusion of electronic elements like video clips would enable these students to master some of the skills more independently and will lessen the burden on lecturers and Academic Coordinators (ACs). As part of the blended learning approach, it has been decided to involve the resource centre staff (librarians as well as assistants) in the technology support for students. Capacity building and equipping them with tablets has already begun and will be explored and implemented in the second semester.

The responses to the question regarding the need for an LMS indicate that 87% of the lecturers are of the opinion that it is necessary.

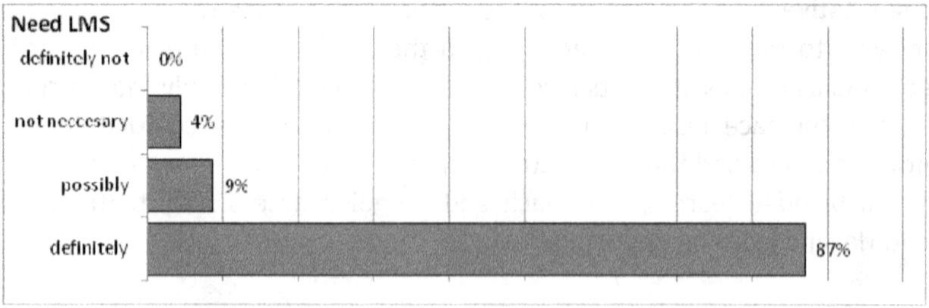

Figure 17: The need for an LMS

The implementation of an LMS or another support platform is therefore undeniably urgent.

Forty-seven of the 69 lecturers (68%) who completed the questionnaire suggested that an alternative device should replace the tablets currently in use.

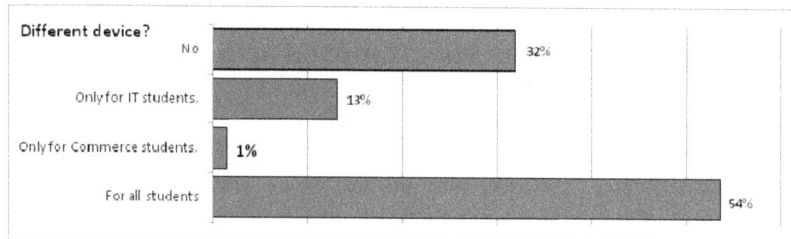

Different device?

No	32%
Only for IT students.	13%
Only for Commerce students.	1%
For all students	54%

Figure 18: The need for a different device

Functionalities that are deemed necessary include the following:

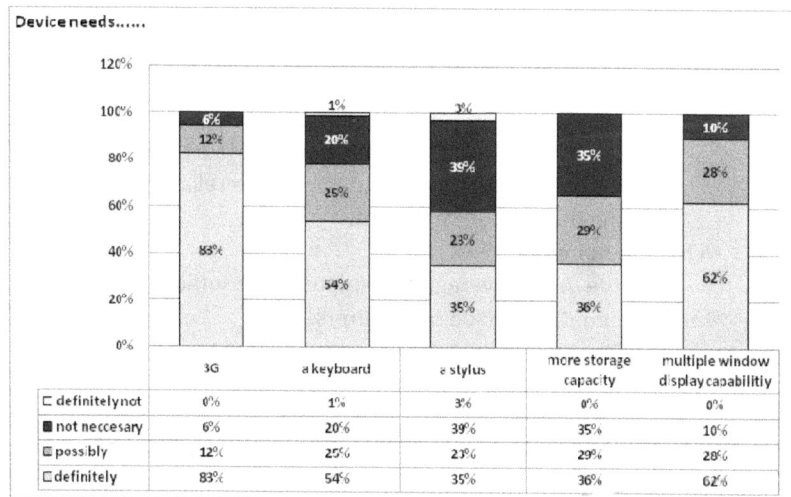

Device needs......

	3G	a keyboard	a stylus	more storage capacity	multiple window display capabilitiy
definitely not	0%	1%	3%	0%	0%
not neccesary	6%	20%	39%	35%	10%
possibly	12%	25%	23%	29%	28%
definitely	83%	54%	35%	36%	62%

Figure 19: Functionalities requested for device

The need for a device with 3G connectivity is the most urgent and was requested by 83% of the lecturers who completed the questionnaire. This problem is purely hardware related and fairly easy to solve. The next two needs, namely those for a device with a keyboard and multiple window display capability, are possible to overcome by using the device more often and improving the skills needed. The need for a device with more storage capacity can be overcome by replacing the current device by one that has a USB port.

6 Recommendations and proposed actions

As mentioned earlier in this report, four categories of problems experienced by lecturers regarding the use of tablets and e-books for teaching and learning were identified. These categories are as follows: In the first place, infrastructure, secondly and thirdly device and software specific requirements and preferences and finally implications for teaching and learning. The following actions have either already been taken or are currently being investigated.

6.1   Upgrade campus networks and Wi-Fi coverage

This specific aspect was repeatedly addressed through lecturers' reactions and answers to all three questions asked at the RDSs and the RI:

- **What worked?**
    - o   The distribution of material through the campus network and the active engagement of students by the use of Internet in class worked well. The success of both of these activities is dependent on the reliability of the infrastructure on campuses.
- **What did not work?**
    - o   The Wi-Fi coverage on campuses is insufficient.
- **Recommendations made by lecturers**
    - o   The recommendation most made was to upgrade the Wi-Fi coverage and campus infrastructure.

It can be reported that the upgrade to increase the number of access points and accommodate more concurrent users has already been completed. Details are available from Russell Lang at CTI GHO (russellhl@cti.co.za).

6.2 Pearson eText: Books and applications (software problems)

This academic semester (second semester: July–November 2013), CTI is only using two Pearson eText books and they are available in e-pdf format on the campus network. We need to consider this a more permanent solution until another workable application can be found. Alternative applications are currently being tested by Pearson.

6.3 Alternative device or added functionalities

This request cannot really be ignored and is currently being investigated. One device that seems to be a good replacement is the "Netbook". This device has 3G connectivity, USB ports as well as a keyboard and is smaller than a laptop, which makes it more mobile. However, it cannot be concluded if this need for a different device is a case of preference by lecturers only. The results of the student survey will either confirm or negate this.

6.4 Change in the format and frequency of student training

As discussed in the previous section, this issue is related to late admissions of students and the due date for payment. We have already found some suitable YouTube videos that can be uploaded to the campus networks. The inclusion of this electronic element as part of the training should alleviate some of the concerns about students' lack of digital literacy. Another action that should improve the support for students is the involvement of resource centre staff. Campuses were requested to make at least one device available to the staff in the resource centre. This will enable them to provide more personal support to students that need help with the use of tablets and e-books.

6.5 LMS implementation

An LMS or similar electronic platform is necessary to support on-going blended learning and training. However, it will place more pressure on campuses' infrastructure. For this reason we are delaying a full scale implementation and are investigating some options. Edmodo, an open source application, is currently used by 23 lecturers on many campuses. The request to explore this application is part of the learning tasks for the lecturers participating in the COP in the second semester. "My labs +", a Pearson product, is another alternative that we will start investigating in August. E-portal, a Moodle-based LMS, currently used by Midrand Graduate Institute (MGI) will also be reviewed.

7   Conclusion – from a lecturer perspective

The overall aim of the implementation of tablets and e-books is to improve the quality of education, i.e. improve and transform current, outdated teaching and learning practices. The focus of this part of the research project focused on the professional development of lecturers and the implementation of core characteristics of an engaged and enabling learning environment, such as interaction and collaboration, together with constructive, authentic and goal-directed learning (TIM) in order to achieve better retention, pass and graduation throughput rates of our students and to prepare them for the workplace (increase employability of all CTI students).

The continuous professional development of lecturers to become lifelong learners is essential - more specifically with regards to developing their 21st century teaching skills (including their digital literacy skills such as the use of social media and educational technologies) and providing them with ongoing support in a technology-enhanced learning environment are some of the critical pillars to ensure successful implementation of new technologies such as e-books and tablets in the learning environment.

There were five important factors identified during the first semester, of which the most important two were that of insufficient IT infrastructure and associated bandwidth and connectivity. Based on some interviews and critical feedback already received during the first part of the first semester from lecturers and students (before the finalisation of this research report), we already had to implement "interim" solutions to ensure better user experiences on campuses from the start of the second semester (although unfortunately not all campuses could be upgraded before the start of the second semester).

Sufficient IT infrastructure, together with the smooth downloading of Pearson eText books to be available offline and off campus, as critical factors for the overall successful implementation of this project and the further roll-out of tablets and e-books to all first year students on all CTI and

MGI campuses at the beginning of 2014, must be highlighted and be given the highest priority. The remaining three factors that were identified from the lecturers' perspective of the research project that have an influence on the optimal implementation of tablets and e-books namely the choice of device and software, as well as the perceived influence of tablets on teaching and learning, the format of lecturer and student training and support as well as the implementation of an LMS have already been communicated to the relevant people and where possible being addressed and further explored. The further roll-out of this project in the second semester, based on the flexible approach in the form of Design-based research will continue and is essential for further and ongoing developments and overall improvement of efficacy.

References

Bennet, S., Maton, K., & Kervin, L. (2008). The digital natives debates: a critical review of evidence. *British Journal of Educational Technology, 39*(5), 775-786.

Lautenbach, G. V. (2011, October 12). Expansive learning cycles: Lecturers using educational technologies for teaching and learning. Johannesburg, Gauteng, South Africa.

Lautenbach, G. V. (2011). *Student-generated design principles for transforming an educational technology module.* University of Johannesburg, Department of Mathematics, Science, Technology & Computer Education. Johannesburg: University of Johannesburg.

Leont'ev, A. (1974). The problem of activity in psychology. *Soviet Psychology, 13*(2), 4-33.

Madyarov, I. (2008). *Contradictions in a distance content-based English as a foreign language course: Activity theoretical perspective.* USF Graduate School. Graduate School Theses and Dissertations.

Nakamaru, S. (2011). *Making (and not making) connections with Web 2.0 technologies.* National Council of Teachers of English.

Reeves, T. C., Herrington, J., & Oliver, R. (2005). Design Research: A socially Responsible Approach to Instructional Technology Research in Higher Education. *Journal of Computing in Higher Education, 16*(2), 96-111.

Rhodes, N. (2012). *Accounting education: Closing the gap between Technology, Education and Accounting in Higher Education Institutions.* Johannesburg: University of Johnnesburg.

Stetsenko, A. (2008). From relational ontology to transformative activist stance on development and learning: Expanding Vygotsky's (CHAT) project. *Cult Stud of Sci Educ*, 471-491.

Stoerger, S. (2009). The digital melting pot: Bridging the digital native-immigrant divide. *First Monday, 14*(7).

Tapscott, D. (2009). *Grown Up Digital: How the Net Generation Is Changing Your World.* McGraw-Hill.

Negotiating the Triple Helix: Harnessing Technology for Transformation

Maggie Hutchings[1], Anne Quinney[1] and Kate Galvin[2]
[1]**Faculty of Health & Social Sciences (HSS), Bournemouth University, Bournemouth, UK**
[2]**Faculty of Health & Social Care, University of Hull, Hull, UK**
Originally published in the Proceedings of ICEL 2014

Editorial commentary

Hutchings et al examine a disruptive pedagogy course and analyse the issues of changing culture at the level of student, teacher and organization. Often underestimated, change management is crucial to successful disruptive innovations, especially in the educational sector. Indeed, education touches upon institutionalized practices such as teaching in traditional classrooms and lecture halls, where teachers "transmit" "knowledge" to students which is then evaluated by quizzes and exercises. Digital learning has been a destabilising force, flipping classes, creating MOOCs and making it possible to learn "on the go". Technology-driven change has been quick and global. Web 2.0 is only 9 years old; the first iPhone is 7. No time at all compared with our 2,000 years of pedagogy. Even so, this digital revolution has changed everything: the ways teachers teach, the ways students learn and the way an organization functions (infrastructure, culture, cost, roles, etc.). We thus conclude this book with a "triple helix" view of change in an educational setting, an essential component of any eLearning success story.

Abstract: Universities are embracing digital technologies to enhance learning and teaching while endeavouring to maximise the student experience, minimise risks, and manage complex, sometimes competing and contradictory agendas. Government policies are focused on placing students at the heart of the process, but with the propensity for student identities to shift from partners in learning to consumers of education. Higher education institutions (HEIs) are grappling with the potential of technology-enabled solutions to enhance education provision in cost-effective ways without placing the student experience at risk. These pressures impact on academics and educational institutions requiring responses to the pace of change, role transitions, and pedagogical imperatives for student-centred learning. The paper explores strategies for effective change management which acknowledge but minimise risks in technology-enabled approaches for transformative learning. The analysis is informed by the development of a collaborative lifeworld-led, transprofessional curriculum for health and social work disciplines, which harnesses technology to connect learners to humanising practices and evidence based approaches. Rich data from student questionnaires and staff focus groups is drawn on to highlight individual and organisational benefits and barriers, including cultural resistance recognised in staff scepticism and uncertainty, and organisational resistance, recognised in lack of timely and responsive provision of technical infrastructure and support. Intersections between research orientations, education strategies and technology affordances will be explored as triggers for transformation in a 'triple helix' model of change, through examining their capacity for initiating 'optimum disruption' to facilitate student-centred learning, role transitions, and organisational change. We share the findings of 'our story' of change to harness the positive utility of these triggers for transformation through deploying strategies for negotiating complexity, including the requirement for a shared vision, a robust team approach, the need for ongoing horizon scanning and application of soft skills (e.g. active listening, timely communication) necessary in order to build student confidence, academic partnerships, and facilitate organisational dexterity in the face of barriers to change.

Keywords: transformative learning; change management; technology-enabled learning; role transitions; organizational change

1   Introduction

The challenges for universities to survive and prosper in the early 21st century are highlighted by Shore's argument (2010, p.15) that 'a new set of discourses has emerged around universities and their role that draws together different, often contradictory, agendas' heralding 'a shift towards a new, multi-layered conception in which universities are expected to fulfil a plethora of different functions'. Government policy in the UK and other countries exerts its influence, promoting the central role of the university in contributing to the knowledge economy while also seeking greater ac-

Marlena Kruger and Riana Bester

countability and performativity evidenced in a multitude of measured outputs, performance indicators, quality assurance measures and audits
(Olssen & Peters 2005; Shore 2010). In order to survive and prosper within
this complex and competitive climate, HEIs must engage in strategies to
advance research, education and professional practice while seeking to
attract students. These demands impact on individuals and organisations,
requiring the university to negotiate and respond to the pace of change,
role transitions, and pedagogical imperatives for more student-centred
learning which is risk-free for the student experience.

Universities are embracing technological advances to facilitate teaching
and learning, simultaneous with the growing use of mobile and digital
technologies in students' everyday lives. Lea and Jones (2011, p.378) suggest 'the potential of social networking, digital and mobile technologies are
permeating the academy, not only through student practice but in terms of
dominant institutional drivers and government-led funding to harness
technologies and applications for supporting teaching and learning'. Technology-enabled approaches offer potential for enhancing student learning
within the complexity and demands of HE provision by crossing boundaries
between research and practice, creating opportunities for co-construction
of knowledge, and releasing academic staff potential to engage with a re-
balanced workload in research, education, and professional practice. While
change in higher education is endemic, technology-enabled initiatives can
contribute to the complexity and pace of these changes. These developments require detailed organisational planning, co-ordination and resourcing (Breen et al 2001) to assure effective change management and minimise risks. This is not to suggest that change can be managed scientifically
in a rational, ordered and linear fashion with appropriate planning tools
and resources in place. The reality of change may be experienced by different stakeholders as an amalgam of more disjointed and disruptive processes. Initiators of technology enabled approaches, offering new mixes of
tutor-facilitated and student-managed learning, can encounter resistance
to change manifested at individual and organizational levels where these
developments challenge deeply held beliefs and pedagogic practices
(Greener 2009, 2010a. p.188).

2   Theoretical framework

Research tends to concentrate on benefits and outcomes rather than examining evidence of processes and people at work in the disjuncture, flux and movement within education initiatives. Pennington (2003, p.4) highlights the tensions between outcomes and process orientations:

> *Structures, procedures, attitudes and behaviours underpinning the status quo have often taken years to lay down and are not susceptible to overnight transformations. For this reason the introduction and management of change should be conceived as a rolling process requiring subtle and persistent choreography rather than a defined event occurring at a particular moment.*

We believe the notion of the positive utility of resistance to change should not be overlooked and can be explored and better understood in order to implement change successfully. Understanding transformative learning at individual and organizational levels, and acknowledging and working with resistance, reluctance and pedagogic diversity is at the heart of negotiating change creatively and sensitively. This position acknowledges the importance of context and situated learning (Argyris & Schön 1978, Lave & Wenger 1991) and builds on constructivist (Mayes & Freitas 2007) and experiential learning theory (Dewey 1933, 1938). The utility of generating purposeful disruptions as tensions and challenges to stimulate transformative learning has been considered elsewhere (Hutchings, Scammell & Quinney 2013). While recognising the value of education initiatives as levers for transformation and organisational change, we also recognise the challenges for change agents in attempting to achieve 'optimum disruption' where initiatives are experienced as too uncomfortable, too difficult or simply too unwelcome and therefore resisted or rejected (Hutchings, Quinney & Scammell 2010a).

This paper shares 'our story' of negotiating change in the development of a collaborative lifeworld-led transprofessional curriculum for health and social work disciplines. Our purpose is to explore the intersections between three strands, (1) research orientations, (2) education strategies, and (3) technology enabled learning, described as the 'triple helix', through their capacity for initiating 'optimum disruption' towards both transforming the student learning experience and academic and organisational cultures (See

Figure 1). We will examine strategies deployed for negotiating complexity, including the requirement for a shared vision, a robust team approach, the need for ongoing horizon scanning and application of soft skills (e.g. active listening, timely communication) necessary in order to build student confidence, academic partnerships, and facilitate organisational dexterity in the face of barriers to change.

3 Case study

Exploring Evidence to Guide Practice (EE2GP) is an undergraduate intermediate (Level I, Year 2) unit/module designed for large student cohorts. Technology is used to connect learners to humanising practices and evidence based approaches. Students are encouraged to integrate different kinds of complex knowledge and consider how their practice could be guided in such a way as to achieve transformative learning. Key drivers for this major development were informed by the University's and Faculty's strategic priorities to:

- Expose undergraduate students to research undertaken in the Faculty of Health and Social Sciences (HSS) and bringing research and teaching cultures closer together
- Pioneer the application of innovative teaching, learning and assessment strategies
- Increase usage of technology enabled learning
- Release staff potential; by achieving economies of scale through replacing face-to-face teaching across all the professional programmes with one common blended learning module

The scale of transformational change effected by this initiative was considerable with anticipated and unanticipated outcomes. Key challenges associated with changing cultures, managing the scale of technology infrastructure, support required, and raised expectations for learning technology provision, were highlighted at individual, Faculty and organization levels. Since the curriculum was introduced in 2010, 11 professional groups have been involved with over 600 undergraduate students each year from nursing (adult, child health, learning disabilities and mental health), midwifery, occupational therapy, physiotherapy, operating department practice, paramedic science, community development and social work. The initiative impacted directly on working practices, within HSC and the wider University. Key stakeholders included, academics, programme leaders, the Faculty's management team, and professional staff in advisory and support roles, based in the Faculty and centrally, including a web developer/educational technologist, learning technologist, IT project manager, academic staff developer, quality and enhancement officer, and examinations coordinator. Approximately 40 academic staff have contributed to the module as developers, champions and facilitators. Introducing this module as a large change management initiative necessitated the negotiation of barriers and risks associated with resistance to change and some scepticism in our Faculty, not dissimilar to the 'resentment and ambiguity' identified by Browne (2005, p.57).

Triple Helix Model of Change

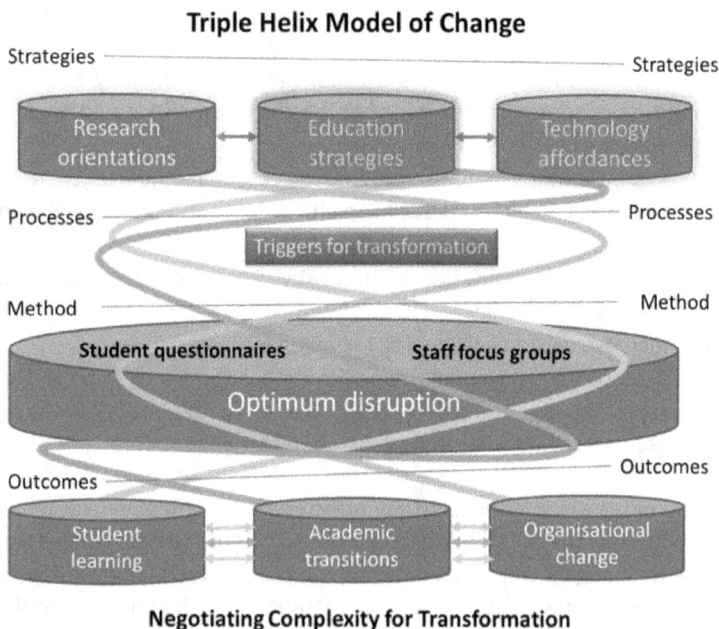

Figure 1: Triple helix model of change: research process and findings

4 Methodology

'Our story' of negotiating change is told through the voices of those experiencing it, to enable us to explore strategies for effective change management through three major levers for change (the 'triple helix', of research, education and technology) towards transformations recognised in impacts on student learning, academic roles and organisational develop-ment. The methodological approach adopted was to build a multi-authored narrative for our story of negotiating change (See Figure 1). This approach is informed by the concept of 'organizational becoming' (Thomas et al 2011, p.22), where organizations are recognised 'not as fixed entities, but as unfolding enactments' in flux and 'constituted by and shaped from micro-interactions among actors, situated in their every-day work'. Our own position is that levers for optimum disruption towards achieving transformative learning can be recognised in action at individual and or-ganizational levels through student and staff descriptions of their experi-ences. We draw on qualitative data collected in 2010-11 and 2011-12, cap-tured through questionnaires and focus groups, to highlight individual and organisational benefits and barriers in deploying the triple helix (See Table 1).

Table 1: Demographic profile of participants

Data collection method	2011.1 Block 1	2011.2 Block 2	2012.1 Block 1	2012.2 Block 2
Students	n = 306	n = 260	n =219	n = 302
Online evaluation questionnaire 15 item statements 5-point Likert scale (Strongly agree to strongly disagree)	n = 301	n = 243	n = 188	n = 283
5 Open response questions				
What enhanced learning	Student 2	Student 1, 9, 10		
What challenged learning		Student 8, 13, 18, 20	Student 4, 6	
What you enjoyed most	Student 3, 7, 14			
What you enjoyed least	Student 12, 15, 17	Student 5, 19	Student 11	Student 16
Response rate	98%	94%	86%	94%
Staff				
Focus group (SFG) Horizon scanning tool	n = 12			

The student experience was monitored and evaluated through weekly deployment of questions using the ARS (audience response voting system) and an end of module online evaluation completed following their online exam. A staff focus group (n=12) was conducted with academic champions and developers interested in contributing to the module, using an horizon scanning tool to stimulate discussions. Further staff comments were captured during a launch event and through ongoing feedback from programme teams. The core project team also shared their experiences of developing the module, considering what it meant for them, and how they engaged with the ups and downs of the process. The analysis of this data informs this paper. Ethical processes were followed to ensure informed consent and data confidentiality in compliance with institutional protocols for undertaking educational research with students and staff.

5   Analysis of findings

The intersections between research, education strategies and technology with their capacity for initiating 'optimum disruption' are examined in relation to achieving student-centred learning, academic role transitions, and organisational change. These complex interrelationships forced us to consider issues of interdependency, tensions and, at times, conflicting agendas in respect of changing cultures, organizational priorities and our core team goals.

5.1   Research for practice

A key driver for the initiative was to expose undergraduate students to research undertaken in the Faculty by drawing on research expertise informed by a lifeworld-led philosophy (Galvin & Todres 2013). 17 web-based case studies were developed to provide diverse evidence of people's experiences of specific illnesses and conditions, such as stroke, dementia, or social isolation. Students were facilitated to explore a range of evidence from the arts and humanities including narratives and poems, informed by citizen and service user perspectives, in association with qualitative and quantitative research papers, and policy documents, to guide practice for humanly sensitive care (Pulman et al 2012).

5.1.1 Student experiences

Students appreciated the relevance of different kinds of research evidence for their practice and the value of engaging with service user and carers' stories:

> Watching the clips relating to my case study, discovering what people went through and it having an impact on my way of thinking and how I can use this within my practice. (Student 1)

> The qualitative evidence stood out for me as I began to empathise with the patients. I was able to understand their thoughts and feelings, and began thinking of how this can be applied to practice. (Student 2)

Students demonstrated developing awareness and confidence to assess different kinds of research evidence and apply critical judgement in professional practice:

> It made me realise that not all evidence is reliable and encouraged me to make my own decision about what evidence to take into account and how to apply it into practice. (Student 3)

However some students experienced difficulties understanding research methodologies and terminology and seeing the application to professional practice. They described varying degrees of disruption from feeling challenged to experiencing the tipping point beyond optimum disruption:

> Getting to understand all of the research terms that I had never heard of before and relating these to practice challenged my learning and has given me a deeper interest into the subject of using evidence to guide practice. (Student 4)

> The amount of reading you were expected to do, and learning all the research processes was incredibly difficult as this topic was totally alien to me. (Student 5)

5.1.2 Staff experiences

This initiative offered opportunities to develop greater integration between research interests and teaching in the Faculty. Academic staff feedback welcomed the integration of lifeworld-led theoretical perspectives for guiding practice:

> *I just really loved the idea that the evidence comes from the arts and humanities as well as the sort of traditional research evidence. (SFG)*

Academic staff also appreciated how the module demonstrated success in bringing the research and teaching cultures closer together:

> *Students have often said to me they think that research is done by those people who are very academic and very senior, so I think it's really good that those people are actually teaching at an undergraduate level and making it applicable to practice in a really exciting way. (SFG)*

However staff also realised the disruptive nature of this approach for their own roles.

> *The model of the unit challenges the traditional way in which we have viewed how we carve out our time as academics and teachers. I'd quite like to develop a case study so how does that fit with my role in the rest of the world of my work, it's not a case of contact hours, but it's about what role do I play? (SFG)*

5.2 Education strategies for change

Another driver was to pioneer the application of innovative teaching, learning and assessment strategies to alter the typical mix of face-to-face lectures and seminars linked to essays or group presentations and encourage more active co-construction of knowledge over information transmission (Hutchings 2008). The student learning experience was facilitated over five weeks with one day contact and one day student managed guided learning each week. Students were allocated an online case study on a particular condition or situation relevant to their professional practice, research process information, podcasts, keynote lectures, and group work activities shared through group blogs. The development of new assessment strategies, including assessment of group blogs, and delivery of a multiple choice computer assisted assessment, has been discussed elsewhere (Hutchings et al 2013).

5.2.1 Student experiences

Students had to read, prepare weekly blogs and work in groups to produce their group coursework summary. They recognised the student centred learning approach as different and some enjoyed the active and collaborative learning opportunities:

> *It is the first time that we have really had to manage our own learning rather being 'fed' the information in a lecture. (Student 6)*

> *I enjoyed working in my group to produce the final blog. We worked well together and were able to bounce ideas off each other. (Student 7)*

The degree of scaffolding necessary to support student learning varied with different students. The challenges were viewed positively by some and they were able to learn progressively using the online resources and guidance:

> *Having to read, understand and submit a blog weekly challenged me and was good for me to take in what I had learned and read and think about it. (Student 8)*

> *The case studies and podcasts have been a new way of learning for me and it has encouraged me to do work on a weekly basis. This is something I usually struggle to do, but knowing that a weekly piece of work needs to be submitted has aided my learning. (Student 9)*

> *Each week it became easier to understand what was required of us to do. It all came together like a jigsaw bit by bit. I felt at the end I had learnt a lot more than I had thought. (Student 10)*

Other students were more reliant on face-to-face contact with a tutor and peers:

> *I would have preferred normal group seminars where we are being taught information and we can freely ask questions. (Student 11)*

The normal pattern of engagement in lectures and seminars appeared to be disrupted by this more independent student managed learning approach, which relied on student engagement and learning with the online materials and guidance provided. The tipping point in optimum disruption, the transition to a more independent learning approach, proved too much for some students.

> *Not being told the information that was necessary to pass the unit, having lecturers believe that "it's on MyBU" or "listen to the podcast" is a suitable response or solution to a student's enquiry. (Student 12)*

5.2.2 Staff experiences
Implications for academic staff were also manifested through the introduction of these different education strategies. Staff who assisted in the development of the web-based case studies vocalised how it can change how they interact with students. One described how she felt distanced from the body of knowledge she had created and concerned the facilitators would do justice to her work:

> *I feel slightly detached now which has been quite difficult. It's like giving birth...! Well there you go and look after it and make sure that you get across what I want you to get across. (SFG)*

5.3 Technology and logistical impacts
The University and Faculty's strategic priorities included increasing usage of technology mediated learning to enable the student learning experience to be enhanced and provide opportunities for academic staff to engage more fully in learning technology enhancement through championing, developing and facilitating curricular initiatives. It was anticipated the introduction of the module would bring economies of scale in staff facilitation realized through the changing balance between face-to-face teaching and online learning. The large cohorts of students each year were facilitated in two blocks of 300 students using a blend of learning technologies which

included online case study resources, group blogs, computer assisted assessment, online frequently asked questions and a fast feedback forum supplemented by face-to-face lectures, student drop-in sessions, and group work. It also required use of a 300 capacity lecture theatre complex for student contact days, booking of computer labs for online assessment, technical support for facilitation of the ARS voting pads, and provision of a robust and secure online assessment platform for delivery of the online exam.

5.3.1   Student experiences
Students recognised the technology mediated approaches adopted as distinct from previous learning experiences and they welcomed the flexibility they afforded:

> *It was so different from any other module we had done before and was highly computer based. (Student 13)*

> *I enjoyed the self-managed learning days as I was able to complete the required work in my own time and at my own pace. (Student 14)*

While some students struggled initially they managed the optimum disruption initiated by these approaches and their readiness for engaging with them improved:

> *I found blogging very difficult as I'm not very brilliant on the computer but that in itself was a learning process! (Student 15)*

> *I think if I was asked to do blogs now I would feel more comfortable with them. (Student 16)*

5.3.2   Staff experiences
The introduction of technology mediated learning within the module affected the roles of academics as developers, champions, and facilitators. It demonstrated role transitions, from module teachers and research staff to resource developers, from uni-professional programme leads to transprofessional champions, and from research-focused professoriate to module facilitators. Academic staff identified how the technology could impact on their working practices and changing roles:

It does radically change how I interact with the students ...... the technology is starting to take us into new areas and there is an element of being de-skilled and wondering how I am going to cope in this brave new world. (SFG)

6   Discussion

We have shared our story and outcomes of working with the complexities of change at individual, professional and organisational levels and identified the connectivity and flux between these levers in securing effective change management. While individual narratives may have focused on the nature of the technology or the education strategies adopted, or the ways the module engaged with research, these findings demonstrate the complexity and intersections of factors at work in successfully managing a major curriculum innovation. They highlight the importance of deploying strategies for change management that can negotiate through the 'wicked' problems (Rittel & Webber 1973), not only logistical but also significantly cultural, and seemingly intractable, which underpin this initiative.

Our analysis has revealed factors identified are as much cultural as logistical. For example, one student says:

I would have preferred more lectures and less 'computerised' study as I don't feel this aided my learning at all. (Student 17)

How are we to interpret this comment? Is this about the use of technology mediated approaches per se or could it be more deeply embedded in the degree of disruption caused by the move away from the normality of educational strategies established in the first year of the programmes and focused on the familiar structure of lecture and seminars? Could the innovation, facilitated through technology enabled learning, have strayed too far from the established culture and personalisation enabled in small face-to-face groups within uni-professional programmes?

I feel this unit has used far too much ICT. I agree it is important in our future disciplines, however, this unit has been completely impersonal. (Student 18)

Studying in such a large group. It lost the personal touch. (Student 19)

On the one hand, organisational level logistical problems in managing complexity, dealing with risks, and achieving integration could be presented as resolvable with careful planning:

There's a lot of quite complex background issues to get resolved and sorted to be able to deliver something that's slick and successful because it requires pulling together an awful lot of different teams. (SFG)
The core planning team acknowledged the need 'to have confidence the technology works' with 'Plans and processes for systems failure and managing organisational pitfalls'. (SFG)

But on the other hand, there was a lot of change impacting on stakeholders at individual and organisational levels. Some staff felt an 'element of being deskilled' with:

So many different techniques and technologies for people who have maybe not engaged in it before. (SFG)

Some students felt overwhelmed by the amount of disruption generated by this initiative:

Having it on a different campus, was all out of our comfort zone, different lecturers, different style of learning, different online style of accessing information. (Student 20)

6.1   Strategies for effective change management
Strategies for success are needed to manage ownership and transferability of the processes and present the key challenge in assuring sustainability of the initiative so that:*'It doesn't sit outside, it sits within'...* (SFG) the programmes, framework teams, Faculty, and University.

6.1.1 Creating a shared vision through a holistic model of change

The success of this initiative is based on a 'triple helix' model of change with three major and interconnected strands, informing, grounding and aligning the processes of change management.

- Strand 1: Research orientation - Embedding a lifeworld-led theoretical perspective as a model of transprofessional learning

The theory of lifeworld led care and education, bringing art and science together, is underpinned and informed by research expertise in the Faculty. Learners are connected to humanising evidence based on the head, heart and hand for guiding and developing professional practice for critical judgement and ethical sensitivity.

- Strand 2: Education strategies - Realising a social-constructivist pedagogy for informing student-centred collaborative learning

Student effort is rewarded through reading, imagining and integrating evidence, capitalising on the significance of others through innovative arts and humanities materials as well as traditional research evidence, peer group learning, and tutors. The key message is that research is embedded in practice and not a technical toolkit. Learning is assessed formatively by means of weekly individual blogs and summatively through group coursework blog summaries and an online multiple choice exam.

- Strand 3: Technology affordances - Harnessing the potential of a range of technologies to enhance student learning

The learning processes are mediated by a virtual learning environment with rich multimedia web-based case studies and collaborative groupwork facilitated through blogs, online assessment and ARS. The technologies can also deliver cost-effective solutions for managing large student numbers and releasing staff time.

This model of change is dynamic, interactive, and integrative. It has enabled us to forge ahead with managing the complexities and uncertainties wrought by change, working with systemic challenges beyond our control but not beyond the powers of a cohesive and committed team to negotiate and influence.

Marlena Kruger and Riana Bester

6.1.2 Building a robust and dedicated core team for managing change

We have described our approach to change management as 'middle-grounded' to signify the benefits of actively promoting and building on open, flexible, morphing teams, grounded in a humanising philosophy and a shared vision and values for developing innovative pedagogical practices endorsed by our Faculty (Hutchings et al 2011). The shared vision, commitment and complementary team roles helped manage the integration and risks associated with changing cultures, and negotiating institutional processes, technology infrastructure, and raised expectations. Team members drew on the experience, enthusiasm and commitment of colleagues to deal effectively with challenges, constraints and uncertainties associated with the development of this complex project.

6.1.3 Managing organisational challenges through partnership, listening and regular communication

Harnessing technology for enhancing student learning highlighted organisational and individual challenges in managing the changes associated with the scale of technology infrastructure, support required, and emergent expectations for learning technology provision for all. Smith (2012) emphasises the considerations underpinning the diffusion of innovative learning and teaching practices, requiring senior management support, recognition of the time resources needed to change existing practices, supportive networks and institutional infrastructure. Organisational challenges included managing timetabling logistics, organising groupwork rooms and computer labs for online exams, and overcoming systems failures. Working in close collaboration with committed and responsive IT champions helped manage organizational resistance.

Pennington (2003, p.5) recognised that: "Organisational politics are heightened and amplified during a change process as individuals and groups perceive shifts in power, authority, influence and territory. For this reason successful change requires not just technical competence from 'managers', but also sensitivity to political and human dimensions of organisational life." The core team experienced cultural resistance communicated in staff scepticism and uncertainty expressed by professional programme colleagues. These challenges highlighted the importance of promoting ownership and transferability through developing creative and col-

159

laborative partnerships working in flexible and supportive multi-disciplinary/professional teams where roles merge and coalesce. The team's efforts to consider the pedagogic and structural challenges (Browne 2005) in an integrated way were evident in the collaborative team approach, with role transitions experienced by staff being not dissimilar to those identified by Anderson (2009). While it was important to recognize the behaviours, motives and beliefs of staff who may resist change (Outram 2004), the commitment to fostering an effective collaborative team, both within and across discipline areas, assisted in the process of achieving the strategic goals of the university and realizing the vision of the team designing and delivering this module. This approach was intended to avoid what Ward et al (2010 p.40) describe as situations where 'IT-driven decisions and project management principles overrode the pedagogical considerations and autonomy of academic decisions making processes'.

6.1.4 Capitalising on networking opportunities and forming alliances for horizon scanning

Opportunities to network with and learn from colleagues with expertise in different disciplines and other HEIs facilitated through the UK HEA Enhancement Academy (Hutchings et al 2011) provided a powerful and influential resource to inform and support the project. Links established with the University of Oxford Medical Sciences Division proved invaluable for informing the computer assisted assessment. The contribution of a Leadership Foundation for Higher Education (LFHE) 'critical friend' was pivotal in providing focused advice and support and instrumental in 'winning hearts and minds'. The generosity of these colleagues sharing their expertise was highly valued and brought added caché and gravitas to the initiative.

7 Conclusions

We successfully introduced a generic structure and processes through the design and development of this module. As a result, we hope the path for future developments will be made easier for other enthusiasts to follow. In placing pedagogy, informed by a lifeworld-led philosophy and supported by a range of technologies, at the centre of the rationale for change this collaborative and creative project challenged and moulded existing organisational and individual practices (Browne 2005). Our views resonate with those of Greener (2010) that a more detailed understanding is needed of beliefs and behaviours of students and staff and environments in which these operate when introducing and adopting technology enabled learning practices. This incorporates consideration of personal and institutional pedagogies, digital skills and self-efficacy in technology usage. Achieving 'optimum disruption' (Hutchings et al 2010a) requires institutions and individuals to accept the normality of what Ashcraft and Trethewey (2004 p81) refer to as the 'dualities, contradictions and paradoxes' embedded in day to day practices. This can lead to practices that foster the innovation, creativity and change (Barge et al 2008) at the heart of our 'triple helix' model of change.

Acknowledgements

Development and evaluation was supported by the HEA Discipline-focused Learning Technology Enhancement Academy (Hutchings et al 2011) and project funding from JISC/SEDA Embedding Work-with-IT (Hutchings et al. 2010b).

References

Argyris, C. & Schön, D. (1978) *Organizational learning: a theory of action perspective.* Reading, Massachusetts: Addison-Wesley.

Anderson JK. (2009) The work-role transition of expert clinician to novice academic educator. *Journal of Nursing Education*, 48(4) pp 203-208.

Ashcraft KL and Trethewey A. (2004) Developing tension: an agenda for applied research on the organisation of irrationality. *Journal of Applied Communication Research*, 32, pp 302-332.

Barge J K, Le M, Maddux K, Noabring R and Townsend B. (2008) Managing dualities in planned change initiatives. *Journal of Applied Communication Research*, 36 (4) pp 364-390.

Breen R. Lindsay R, Jenkins A and Smith P. (2001) The role of information and communication technologies in a university learning environment. *Studies in Higher Education*, 26 (1) pp 95-114.

Browne E. (2005) Structural and pedagogic change in further and higher education: a case study approach. *Journal of Further and Higher Education*, 29 (1) pp 49-60.

Dewey, J. (1933) *How we think.* Boston: D.C.Heath.

Dewey, J. (1938) *Experience and education.* New York: Simon & Schuster.

Galvin, K. and Todres, T. (2013) *Caring and well-being: a lifeworld approach.* Abingdon: Routledge.

Greener S. (2009) Talking online: reflecting on online communication tools. *Campus-Wide Information Systems*, 26 (93) pp178-190.

Greener, S. (2010a) Staff who say no to Technology Enhanced Learning. *In*: Ismail I (ed). *Proceedings of the 5th International Conference on E-Learning*, Penang, Malaysia. pp 134-139.

Greener S. (2010b) Plasticity: the online learning environment's potential to support varied learning styles and approaches. *Campus-Wide Information Systems.* 27 (4) pp 254-262.

Hutchings, M. (2008) Quick-fix learning: challenging the concept of learning for learning's sake. In Rust, C. (ed.) *Improving Student Learning: For What?* Oxford Centre for Staff Development. pp 143-57.

Hutchings, M., Quinney, A. and Scammell, J. (2010a) The Utility of Disruptive Technologies in Interprofessional Education: Negotiating the Substance and Spaces of Blended Learning, *In* Bromage, A. et al. (Eds) *Interprofessional eLearning and Collaborative Work: Practices and Technologies.* Hershey, PA: IGI. pp 190-203.

Hutchings, M., Galvin, K., Todres, L., Quinney, A., Pulman, A., Atkins, P. and Gentle, P. (2010b) *Transformational Change through Lifeworld-led Multimedia VLE engagement*, Embedding Work-with-IT Final Report. Bournemouth University and the Leadership Foundation for Higher Education for JISC/SEDA.

Hutchings, M., Galvin, K., Pulman, A., Todres, L., Quinney, A., Clark, V. and Atkins, P. (2011) *Framing Lifeworld-led Evidence to Shape Practice: Facilitating a Collaborative Transprofessional Curriculum for Health and Social Work Disciplines.* Final Report for Higher Education Academy Discipline-focused Learning Technology Enhancement Academy. Bournemouth University.

Hutchings, M., Quinney, A., Galvin, K. and Clark, V. (2013a) The yin/yang of innovative technology enhanced assessment for promoting student learning. In Greener, S. (ed.) *Case studies in e-learning research for researchers, teachers, and students.* Reading: Academic Publishing International. pp 62-79.

Hutchings, M., Scammell, J. & Quinney, A. (2013b) Praxis and reflexivity for interprofessional education: towards an inclusive theoretical framework for learning. *Journal of Interprofessional Care* 27 (5) pp 358-366.

Lave, J. & Wenger, E. (1991) *Situated learning: legitimate peripheral participation.* Cambridge: Cambridge University Press.

Lea M R and Jones S. (2011) Digital literacies in higher education: exploring textual and technological practice. *Studies in Higher Education,* 36 (94) pp 377-393.

Olssen, M. & Peters, M.A. (2005) Neoliberalism, higher education and the knowledge economy: from the free market to knowledge capitalism. *Journal of Education Policy* 20 (3) pp.315-345.

Outram S. (2004) 53 interesting ways in which colleagues resist change. *Educational Developments*, 5 (2) pp 1-4.

Pennington, G. (2003) *Guidelines for promoting & facilitating change.* Higher Education Academy: Learning and Teaching Support Network Generic Centre.

Pulman, A.J., Galvin, K., Hutchings, M., Todres, L., Quinney, A., Ellis-Hill, C. and Atkins, P. (2012) Empathy and Dignity through Technology: using Lifeworld-led

Multimedia to Enhance Learning about the Head, Heart and Hand. *Electronic Journal of E-Learning*, 10 (3) pp.320-330.

Rittel, H.W.J. and Webber, M.M. (1973) Dilemmas in a general theory of planning. *Policy Sciences* 4 pp 155-169.

Shore, C. (2010) Beyond the multiversity: neoliberalism and the rise of the schizophrenic university: Special issue on anthropologies of university reform. *Social Anthropology* 18 (1) 15-29.

Smith K. (2012) Lessons learnt from literature on the diffusion of innovative learning and teaching practices in higher education. *Innovations in Education and Teaching International*, 49 (2) pp 173-182.

Thomas, R. Sargent, L.D. and Hardy, C. (2011). Managing organizational change: negotiating meaning and power-resistance relations. *Organization Science* 22 (1) pp.22-41.

Ward M-H, West S, Peat M and Atkinson S. (2010) Making it real: project managing strategic e-learning development processes in a large, campus-based university. *Journal of Distance Education,* 24 (1) pp 21-42.